Living Life as an ADVENTURE

BOOK 1

BY ESTHER DAVIS LANG

LIVING LIFE AS AN ADVENTURE
BOOK 1

ISBN (Paperback): 979-8-89672-100-0
ISBN (Ebook): 979-8-89672-101-7

Cover design: Sydney Lang
Editing and production: Daryl Lang

Printed in the United States of America.

PROMINENT
BOOKS
EDGE

5830 E 2nd St, Ste 7000 #9983
Casper, WY 82609
USA

Introduction

Family and friends or whoever decides to be bored and reads this, pretend we are having dinner at my house. We are enjoying a delicious pot roast with potatoes, and carrots, and onions, and raised dumpling with lots of gravy. My Mother used to make the dumplings from scratch but I'm afraid this is made with Bisquick. There will be Joanne's cherry cobbler for dessert.

Read this as if I am talking to you. Ignore the grammar. It's the way I talk.

Contents

Prologue

It must have been love. How else can one explain why a debutante from the university town of Delaware, OH., marries a farmer's son from the mountains of West Virginia. Well, that is exactly what happened back in 1922, and that is the prologue to my life.

My father, Delbert Davis, thought he would become a Methodist minister and went to Ohio Wesleyan University to fulfill that ambition. There he met the debutante, Esther Buck, a doctor's daughter. He was quite the man with words and though he went off to war 1917 he courted her through letters. He did not return to OWU, but did continue the letters. (I found one among my Mother's things.) They were married in June 1922 and moved to Gormania W VA., where he was cashier (back then the cashier was the boss) of the First National Bank of Gormania. She was The Banker's Wife. They lived in the apartment over the bank. (she told me she did the laundry in the bath tub, can you imagine?). I can't recall her ever wishing to be anywhere but with him.

Chapter 1 • 1924, Childhood

"Life can be a great adventure
If you choose to live it like a Great Adventure."
—Anonymous

So... it was on August 1, 1924 when I first opened my eyes to this great big wonderful world... (oh sure, I remember it well!?!). I was at the Farm House of my grandparents, David & Lily Orum Davis. My Aunt Beryl, their daughter, was living there also.

It happened like this...

My father was cashier of the First National Bank of Gormania, W VA. Gormania was located on the W VA. side of the Potomac River. My Dad's parents lived in Gorman, across the river, on the Maryland side. My folks were living in an apartment over the bank when my brother, Delbert Maurice Jr., was born on April 4, 1923. He was 6 months old when

My Dad and grandfather at the farm.

they moved to the farm where I was born. Dad was moving up in the banking world and became cashier of The First National Bank of Oakland. Oakland was the county seat of Garrett County, Maryland. It was a good move up for my Dad.

I was 8 months old when we moved to a brandnew cinder block house on Liberty St, in Oakland. My Mother must have been in her glory, moving from, first, the apartment over the bank where she had to do her laundry in the bathtub, and then with inlaws at the farm. That little house must have been a dream fulfilled. It was 2 stories with a basement. The first floor held the kitchen, dining room and a larger front room. On the 2nd floor were 3 bedrooms and a bath. After

much conversation with my brother, there seems to be no record of the "how and why" my grandparents moved to Oakland. We know my grandfather did not own the farm in Gorman. He leased and

farmed it until an arsonist set fire to the barn, killing the horses and other animals. We think he had previously owned a farm in Pleasant Valley. We think he sold that farm and possibly with that money bought the property in Oakland. (All presumption.) Or maybe he and Dad, together, bought the five lots we lived on. There was an empty lot on each side of our house, then my Grandpa's house and then another empty lot. The lot between the two houses was the garden. How my Dad loved to garden! What is it they say, "you can take the farmer out of the farm but you can't take the farm out of the farmer"? There was always a garden wherever he settled.

The lot on the other side of our house had Mother's rock garden. Her pride and joy! There were stepping stones leading down to the street. About half way down was the fish pond. A concrete hole in the ground that housed one goldfish. Believe it or not that fish hibernated during the winter and was good to go when the ice melted.

There was a garden club in Oakland and Mother worked hard to win a prize when some contest was run, but I don't remember her ever winning anything.

When does one first recollect life's goings on? My first recollections are of Maurice and I walking the path across the garden to my Grandparent's house and Grandma giving us cookies. I remember Maurice & I playing in the manure pile in the garden and getting a whipping for it. (It was always Maurice's ideas that got us into trouble!?!?)

Grama + Grandpa's back Porch
me Gramma Mother, Maurice, Grandpa

Maurice and I shared a bedroom (2 twin beds), when we were little. We were only 18 months apart, and were pretty much matched in size and strength. We would wrestle and sort of fight. I could hold my own for a few years (I was a real Tom Boy), but Maurice was a tease, and never knew when to stop. One time he held me under the covers, I couldn't breathe, and panicked. Guess that is when I became claustrophobic.

He was a tease but he was also a scaredy cat. The stairs to the second floor had a landing, then 3 more steps to the hallway. When it was dark, Maurice would always ask me to go up ahead of him.

One day, Maurice and some neighbor kids and I were walking home from school when another kid started to give us a bad time. I hauled off and socked him! Apparently, after that, I was a hero. I was kinda proud of myself, too

I do remember my grandmother quilting. She had all the dining room furniture moved into one corner so she could set up a quilting frame. It stood on legs high enough for her to sit and quilt. There were 2 rollers, one at each end and the quilt was stretched between them. As she worked the quilt was unrolled at one end and rolled up on the end.

They are beautiful quilts! I have two of them; one has baskets of flowers. Each basket has a handle with the name of the flower (that is in the basket) embroidered on it. The other quilt has butterflies

3

with the details of the butterflies embroidered on them I vaguely remember the time my Grandmother died. She, and grandpa had joined Aunt Beryl in Elkins W Va. where Aunty had a job. Gramma was at church when she had a heart attack, dying instantly. (What a way to go!)

While they were in Elkins, they rented their house to the Krause's—a family with 3 children. Jimmy, the oldest, was my age, then Wayne and then Shirley. What fun—new playmates! We would play "Run Sheepey Run" or "Mother, may I?"

I remember their father was very strict and would beat them with his belt. Their mother was nice, though, and became our scout leader.

Auntie & Grandpa continued to live in Elkins until he developed some heart condition. I guess he wanted to come back home for Auntie got a job with the Gas Co in Oakland, and they returned to their home (the Krause's moved out.)

It was during this time, after they moved back to Oakland, that I remember most. I would go next door where Auntie taught me to knit, and embroidery and she tried to teach me to Tat, but I never learned. She had me knitting a complete dress—it was pretty blue yarn. I remember I knitted the skirt using round needles.

Grandpa had had some teeth pulled and one day as he was sitting on his porch, I found him scrapping an apple and eating it. He gave me some off his knife. Have you ever eaten scraped apple? Take my word for it—it is so very good!

There was a small potbelly stove in Grandpa's dining room and another in the front room. They were coal hungry and had to be fed at regular intervals. The coal house was out back and every winter the snow would create a big drift along one side of it. One winter, Maurice & I made an igloo into  the drift. It was large enough that we could both crawl into it. We even had a little ledge inside where we could set a candle. We photographed Auntie with her foot and leg in the entrance.

One year a family of skunks took up residency under the coal house. There was quite a stir in the neighborhood, but I can't remember how it was resolved.

One Easter Auntie gave us each a baby chick. One died, but as the other grew, we anxiously waited for it to lay an egg. Then, one morning we were awakened with the crowing of that HEN. So much for eggs. Dad liked to write verses so, of, course, there was a verse about "The Crowing Hen."

That rooster was a feisty one. We had two little girls living next door and that bird would chase them home every time they tried to come & play.

Well, one day grandpa took that 'ole rooster out back and wrung its neck. It is still vivid in my mind how it thrashed around afterward. Mother cooked it but we couldn't eat it.

Brother Maurice had two rabbits. One day as he was cleaning out the hutch, he found a couple of baby mice inside. He called Mother and was ready to scoop them out when she arrived. She quickly noticed they weren't baby mice after all, but baby rabbits. So now we had a full hutch of rabbits. Somehow, they all died but one— Apple Dumpling. He was a big soft furry, black & white dumpling of a rabbit and would hop around the back yard when let out.

He also played the part of the wild animal when we played "circus." We had neighbor children who were always part of our playing, and helped with the circus.

The circus was a big event! Dad had put up a trapeze in the garage. Maurice was good on it and could 'skin the cat', hang by his toes, & do tricks with the rings. Berniece could do all that and hang by her heels too (Maurice was envious). They were the trapeze artists. I could only skin the cat. But I was the Fat Lady! Stanley, Berniece's brother, couldn't do much either. We bought chewing gum in 6 packs cartons for 25 cents then sold the packs for 5 cents each. Big finances. My folks had a young bachelor friend, Judd Loar, who spoiled us children. He always attended our circus and always bought gum. When he visited my folks, he always brought us candy. You can bet, he was always welcome!!

Bernice & Stanley Sines. They were poor! Their father left them and Mrs. Sines took in laundry. Stanley was my age and Bernice was about 4 years older. She & I were great play  mates. We would walk to school together. In the winter, Mother would worry that Bernice didn't dress warmly enough. You see, she had asthma and could hardly breathe. They didn't know what to do for it except burn stuff that was supposed to make breathing easier for her. She and I belonged to Girl Scouts and we went to Scout camp one summer (there is a photo of her and moi in hula skirts). It was sad when she died. She was only 16.

Maurice was always our leader. We would play store using certain wild plants for veggies. I remember there was sour grass for candy, there was a plant that had leaves similar to carrots and clover blossoms were money. When we finished playing, Maurice would gather all the greens and feed them to the rabbit. Smart, uh?

We continued to live on Liberty St, where life was routine, enjoying warm summer days of childhood fun and cold snowy winters of sledding and school.

We always looked forward to the week when Dad had a vacation and we could travel to Canandaigua Lake, N.Y. Dad had an old army buddy who had a cottage on Canandaigua Lake. One of NY's finger lakes. We would pack up the old Willy's Knight (that's a car); suitcases strapped on the back; the

Traveled in this Willys Knight

luggage carrier on the right running board where our pet dog, Coalie, rode and we were off! One year, on the trip there, poor Coalie's foot

6

slipped out of the carrier and dragged on the road. We felt so sorry for him. He had a sore paw for a while, but fully recovered.

There were at least 3 years, that I remember, going to Canandaigua Lake. One year the Whipkey's joined us. The cherry trees were having a bumper crop, that year, so the adults spent a day out picking cherries. There were the usual red cherries, but there were, also, the big black sweet cherries. Uncle Stanton was fussed at for eating more than he put in the bucket. But he had his comeuppance when they were back at the cottage and were pitting the cherries. Every black cherry had a worm in it.

I must have been around 8 years old when Dad bought water front property on Deep Creek Lake. You see, in the late 1920's Western Maryland was growing and there became a need for more electric power. A big hydroelectric power plant was built and a dam

was needed to create the water power. Consequently, a dam was built, a valley was flooded and Deep Creek Lake was formed. There were farms and much wooded area in that valley. I'm sure the farmers were well compensated for their land. (In fact, I remember Dad bought his parcel of land from the Becker's farm.) The trees were all cut for lumber (the lumber mills must have had a field day, too) but the stumps were left behind. The lake front property Dad bought was strewn with stumps.

I clearly remember the stumps, for my Dad and Grandfather dynamited the stumps out of the ground. I can still see those stumps flying into the air. It was scary! We had to stand back and hoped Dad would get back before the dynamite blew. Working with dynamite isn't for amateurs.

The job, after all the stumps were cleared out, was to rake off the stones so we would have a nice sandy beach. Maurice and I did help with that. Then came the dock. It was a platform, probably 6 ft by 12 ft. on old, empty oil barrels that floated. Since the power plant drew water from the lake every summer, the lake shore line would recede. So, the dock had to be pushed out as the water receded. It was tied by two heavy ropes to two trees inland and was accessed by a catwalk, also on a barrel at one end.

There was a boat! A little five ft metal row boat with air seats at each end. It would float right side up or upside down. We would sometimes turn it over and hide under it. Mother and Dad figured we were safe because we could swim. At that time, no one considered Lifejackets or Lifesaving equipment. After all we could swim. Some years later, my little sister was about 3 or 4, Maurice and I took her for a row boat ride. By then the lake had bigger boats and faster boats racing up and down the lake. We were out in our little row boat, Maurice was rowing. Charlotte & I were on the back seat, enjoying the ride and admiring the scenery. All was well, until a speeding boat raced by. Maurice knew to turn the boat nose into the waves but as the waves washed over the boat, they began to sweep Charlotte off the back of the boat. Thank heavens I was able to catch her before she

 was swept overboard. I can't remember how Mother and Dad reacted. Were they concerned, probably not, after all, we could swim. All is well that ends well?

Now, about the cottage itself. I don't know if it went up before or after the work on the shoreline. It was very rustic. It was shingled. It was one big room. A smaller room, the kitchen, and a porch were across the "lake side". The big room had a glorious stone fireplace at one end. The other end was partitioned off with curtains hung on wires. There were 3 areas. The ones to the right and the left had double, double bunks and the one in the middle had a single bed.

There was no electricity. The outside privy had a note on the toilet seat that read, "To save your nose from much abuse, keep this seat down when not in use". Kerosene lamps lit the rooms at night, and kerosene was used in the little portable stove for cooking. Water came from a well just outside the door. There was a pump with the typical pump handle. One just took a pail outside and pumped until it was full of water.

My Dad, still the farmer, named the place Lake Shore 40. It became the family's Jewel.

We always spent Dad's vacation week there, but to help pay the mortgage, it was rented throughout the summer. Every weekend we would drive the 8 miles to the cottage where Mother and Dad would clean up after renters and get ready for the new renters. They always warned the new people to beware the sun. The constant breeze on the lake made the heat from the sun deceiving. Many a renter went home with painful sunburns.

I'm sure all this was hard on my parents, but Maurice and I loved it!! While Mother and Dad were slaving, we were playing in the sand, swimming, boating, picking huckleberries so Mother could

mix up a cobbler and have the neighbor bake it in her oven. The neighbors lived there all year long so had the amenities we didn't. There were 3 children who joined us in our play. Stella was the oldest, Diddy, who was Maurice's age and Bobbie, much younger. They had a boat too, and we would row across the lake and explore the "Haunted house" or take a picnic to the pasture over there. They always took baked bean sandwiches, ug!

As we grew older and more families with children had cottages and we became more adventurous, we decided to swim across the lake to the pasture on the other side. So, followed by a large inboard boat, and several row boats, we did just that.

It was quite the adventure. I felt very proud of myself. Maurice and Stella swam over and back.

I was 10 when our little sister arrived. Just old enough to delight in helping to care for her! Wow a little baby sister! She was named Charlotte Beryl. The Beryl was for my Auntie Beryl who lived next door and was our babysitter.

Brother Maurice often had nightmares and would cry and walk in his sleep. I remember trying to waken him by showing him toy cars, etc. One evening, Mother and Dad were away and Auntie was babysitting us. Auntie and I were in the kitchen, Charlotte was in her high chair, when Maurice came down the steps, walking in his sleep. He walked toward Charlotte saying, in a monotone, "she's mine, she's mine". It was spooky! It gave Auntie quite a start but we soon got him awake and all was well.

I'm sure Auntie fed us cookies and milk afterward.

Maurice was afraid of the dark, too. He would often ask me to go up the stairs ahead of him and turn on the lights. The stairs had a landing before going another 2 steps into the hallway, it was dark.

There was a sort of coat rack on the wall, at the landing. One Christmas Dad invited Auntie to bring her stocking over to hang with ours. Santa would fill it. She did—it was a pajama leg sewed up like a stocking. When she arrived Christmas morning, she found it filled with popcorn. Dad loved jokes.

On June 7,1938 a little brother was added to our family. I was 14 and I remember, we were in Mother's bed room. She was holding the baby and we were all standing around, trying to think of a name for this new baby boy. We had a book of boy's names. We liked "Norman" but why we ever thought Winfred would be a good middle name only the Lord knows. I certainly can't blame him for not liking it.

Norman was still in the buggy age when we moved to Ashberry Manor. It was a big beautiful house situated in the center of a whole city block, on the other side of town. You see, Dad, working in the bank as he did, was privy to things going on around town. When he heard this property was up for sale, he grabbed it.

Oakland was settled along the Little Youghiogheny River that cut a valley between 2 hills (not mountains). Our home on Liberty St was at the top of one hill and the new home was on the opposite hill.

The new home needed some work done on it. So, on Saturdays, the family would go there to get it ready for us to move in. That is, all except Norman and Me. I had to stay home and take care of him! One weekend I rebelled and put Norman in the buggy and wheeled him down one hill and up the other hill so I could be a part of what was going on. That was a really bad idea! I was told to turn around and wheel him back down one hill and up the other back to the Liberty St. home. Funny how I have never forgotten that.

1938-1941 High School Days

Ashberry Manor

We moved to Ashberry Manor that fall of 1938, and we all really loved the new home. It was situated in the middle of a town block with oak trees, buckeye trees, Mountain Ash trees and five gorgeous huge rhododendron bushes. Each a different color.

A basement had to be dug and a coal burning furnace installed. There was room in the basement for a ping pong table. (I became quite good at it, but never won any competitive games because I would always slam the ball on a crucial play and lose the game.)

Mother did laundry, and her summer canning down there. She canned everything. She made the best dill pickles and catsup.

The house had 2 front rooms, each with a fireplace and each with a large, beautiful crystal chandelier. I will never forget those chandeliers, for once a year, I had to climb a step ladder and wash every one of those crystals.

There was a large dining room, too, that also, had a lovely crystal chandelier, but a smaller version of the ones in the front rooms. Mother loved those chandeliers. When they moved to Salisbury, she took the smaller one with her.

Off the dining room was a study with a door that opened to the front room, which in turn had a door that opened to a large porch across the end of the house.

An interesting stairway led up, from both the kitchen and the front room, to the 2nd floor. The 2nd floor had a large bathroom where we could sit in front of a little gas heater while Mother melted Vick on a spoon, so we could inhale it for our stuffy noses. There were 5 bedrooms. Two large bedrooms were above the front rooms and each had a corresponding fireplace. I had one of the large bedrooms and it had a working fireplace! I didn't use it much, though. Too lazy, I guess.

There was a finished 3rd floor and then an attic.

Dad grew a large garden and at harvest time Mother worked hard canning the beans, corn and whatever dad harvested. Mother really did work hard. Not only did she do all this canning she cared for a family of 6 and a big house.

Soon they realized Mother needed help and Annie Durst came to live with us. (She was the daughter of a large farming family.) Annie was never "the hired girl". She was always family and had her special place on the 3rd floor and in our hearts and lives. She lived with us until she went off to become a cadet nurse when WW II began.

Not sure when Bart, Mildred Barton, came to live with us. She was the County Home Demonstration Agent and needed a place to room but not board. She too became one of the family. I remember going with her one night to some sort of meeting. Those county folks had made some maple syrup taffy and gave us some. Have you ever

tasted maple syrup taffy? It is divine! I guess, because it is so very arduous to make, it is not often made. But, what a great treat that was!!

There always seemed to be something going on at our home, so we didn't socialize much outside of our home. We weren't involved or close to any other families with children our ages. My Aunt Georgia and Uncle Stanton Whipkey and cousins Laural Allison (5 years older than I) and Mae Orum (Maurice's age), lived a few blocks away. We weren't close. Though, I remember a few years when we would take turns with holiday dinners. And I guess we went on camping trips together. I don't remember, but have pictures.

*Green House
Dad & Mother*

I do remember Aunt Georgia being a good cook. One day I went there when she was making potato chips. That was before you could buy them in the store. BOY were they GOOD!! They were something special!

Dad was cashier of The First National Bank of Oakland. He was active in Rotary Club and Masons. He climbed the chairs to a high position. He did his civic duty by being on Town Council. After a member of the Md House of Representatives, called Garrett Co. "The Tobacco Road of Maryland", Dad countered with fliers saying "Garrett Co, the Switzerland of Maryland", showing pictures of Deep Creek Lake in summer and winter. That showed them!

Dad taught the men's Bible class at the Methodist church. He was always able to get a heated discussion going. The men enjoyed that.

He didn't much care for parties. His passion was his garden (you can take the farmer out of the farm but not the farm out of the farmer); it was a big garden with every veggie he could find in the Burpee's catalogue. There were rows and rows of green string beans.

My first summer home from school I would pick beans by the bushels and take them to town to Smouse's grocery store and sell them.

Dad built a green house, too, where we all had to troop out to see a special flower that blooms only at night. That was neat!

Then there was Jenny the little cocker spaniel that followed him everywhere, especially when he would don his "cow clothes", pick up the bucket and go milk the cow. Yes, there was a cow too. The wonderful part about having a cow was the extra cream for making ice cream. That, we did frequently. Dad would drive to the "creamery" in town and buy a large chunk of ice. With an ice pick, he would chop off pieces of ice to fill the edges around the ice cream can within the churner, then we would start turning the handle, and turn, and turn and turn. When it got hard to turn Dad would cover it with a piece of burlap to keep it cold.

One day the cow got into a corn patch and had her fill. Dad was worried she would founder, so he chased her around the block. I can still see Dad with a stick driving that cow around the block. It was a quiet street and no traffic.

There was a pig only once. and there was a pony named Dolly. Dad used her to plow the garden. He could ride her but every time I got on her she would lie down.

Most embarrassing!

I remember one time when she was first let out of the barn in the spring, she ran from one end of the field then headed back, mane and tail flying so joyful to be out—but then her nose touched the electric fence and she actually sat back on her haunches. It was a sight to behold.

One day Dolly was tied outside the fence where there was good grass. Maurice noticed she was desperately pulling at the rope trying to get away. He ran out to see what was the matter and discovered she was in a bed of yellow jackets. No wonder she was trying to get away! So, he quickly released the rope and she took off, lickity split. Big brother was the hero of the day! Yes, he did get stung,

I remember sitting at the kitchen table with my Dad as he would discuss some plans for the family. He would always include us kids in family discussions. He would talk to us about what it would cost and how we could pay for it. Guess that is where I learned to keep records and be organized.

My Mother! She was always MOTHER. I never called her Mom until many years later. As I look back, I can appreciate that she was truly an amazing woman! She was a doctor's daughter so probably well situated, living in a college town with lots of culture, then marries a farmer's son from the hills of western Maryland. I don't remember her ever wishing to be otherwise.

Mother had a routine: Mondays were wash day when she would wash clothes, cook starch for Dad's shirts and the pillow cases, and then hang the clothes out on the line. On Tuesday she would iron. She had a catsup bottle with a cork sprinkler in it and would dampen the clothes, roll them up and put them in a bushel basket lined with pretty oilcloth. She would set up the ironing board, set the electric iron on the asbestos pad (irons did not set back on themselves) and, while she was ironing a bushel of damped clothes, she would memorize her Eastern Star lines. She belonged to The Eastern Star and everything was secret, so I never knew what she was learning.

While we were living on Liberty St, I liked to watch Mother cut up a chicken. I would sit on a tall stool near the sink where she worked. As she was cutting, she would explain the different parts of the chicken. Was I preparing for Anatomy classes, even back then?

During my High School days she was always THERE. We weren't close for she was busy with small children and a big house and all that involved. I was certainly not neglected. She would get up in the middle of the night and put hot/cold compresses on my head when I got terrible headaches. She made me pretty dresses. I had a difficult figure—I was short waisted and bought dresses were always long at the waist. So, Mother would buy fabric and adjust the pattern to fit me. Bless her! I learned to sew by her side and have blessed those days many times throughout the years. She always had me tie the knots at the end of each seam. Pure drudgery.

One time, she came home, from a trip with Dad, with a gorgeous Fuchsias evening dress that I could wear to a dance at school. She sent me to the beauty parlor to get a ribbon that matched the dress, braided into the back of my hair. Wow!

We never talked "mother/daughter" stuff or the facts of life, tho, she did give me a book. I learned later that Dad took Maurice to a farm to learn, first hand, the facts of life. Oh, to be a boy. I really resented the limitations of being female. But I did like being female.

The High School was only several blocks from our house. We walked, of course.

On snowy days, when the snow would be knee deep, I would wear ski pants under my dress. When I got to school, I would go in the clock room to remove my coat, hat and my ski pants. Females were not wearing pants back then.

I was not the best student mostly B' s, some C's but very few A's. There were extra activities that I enjoyed. I was an alto in the Glee Club and had some minor parts in some of the dramas. But I did love basketball! Not much of a shooter but a really good guard. We had GIRLS RULEs then, and played only a half court. We would play other schools, like Grantsville & even Frostburg who would always beat us. But the adventure of busing to the other schools was always exciting. My boyfriend was on the boy's basketball team and we would always sit in the back of the bus and hold hands.

As I look back, I see myself as a shy, selfconscious, introverted, selfcentered, teenager going through the pangs of puberty. I felt out of place, not a part of things as the other kids. I was discontented and wanted very much to move on to better things but did not know what those better things might be. Obviously, High School years were not my happiest.

I had a girlfriend, Kathryn Butt. We did a lot of things together. She was an all A's student and, for some reason, she liked me, so we became close friends. We both played basketball and would sometimes referee the girls extramural games during lunch hour. We also worked on the school paper. She was always the alfa one. On one occasion, she was away and I made up the paper. When she returned, she didn't like what I had done and did it all over. I was very hurt and I guess I still feel some resentment.

For some reason, I always felt like an outsider.

Yes, of course, there was a boyfriend, John Mason. Again, as I look back, I thought I was in love but down deep it was the pleasure of having a boyfriend. Every girl needs a boyfriend. And one didn't play the field but went steady to ensure a date. That was the way it was, but I would have liked having boys standing in line wanting to take me to the movies. Anyway, I guess we thought we were an "item" for we met in hallways between classes, we sat together on the basketball bus trip and, yes, we necked. But best of all we loved to dance. We were just kids and thought we were really grownup when John got tickets to a big dance at the Hotel. That was when I wore the fuchsia dress Mother had gotten me. Our "love affair" continued as I went on to college. John got a job at Glenn L Martin, in Baltimore, making war stuff for Great Britain (he couldn't afford to go to college).

That was early 1941. We hadn't yet declared war, but it was soon to come. We were supplying England with arms and other war supplies, so, many of the kids went to work in Baltimore boys and girls alike. My friend, Kathryn lived at a Lutheran Girls boarding house while she worked there.

Then Pearl Harbor exploded and the boys were conscripted or volunteered to join the military. John went into the Marines and we saw each other once on Christmas vacation but otherwise it was a love affair via mail. Along with millions of other girls.

1941, High School graduation year. Now, I could leave the callouses of high school behind me and get on to new adventures.

Chapter 2 • 1941, College Days

"Learn from yesterday, live for today, hope for tomorrow.
The important thing is not to stop questioning."
—Albert Einstein

The summer after I graduated from High School, Mother & Dad and I drove to Ohio (I can't remember to what city, Delaware, maybe) to visit Uncle Edgar & Aunt Mary, Mother's brother. Mother's father, Grandpa Buck, had died and there were things that Mother wanted from his home. We visited one of Mother's friends who had a daughter going to school at Bowling Green State University in Bowling Green Ohio. She was taking Physical Education and there was a swimming pool—my requisite for college.

Physical Education seemed to be my choice, for I didn't really know anything else. I loved basketball and I loved to be active. (As I look back on it, if our high school had offered Home Economics, I probably would have realized I loved the domestic activities too—cooking, sewing, etc. and gone into Home Ec., instead.) But our school only offered Academic, Vocational, or Business. We had no choice for extra courses to learn what we might like to do in our future.

After much family discussion and financial figuring, I was off to BGSU. It was ideal for me, for it had a swimming pool (called a Natatorium). It was a small school, and it was relatively inexpensive ($45 a semester tuition), but… it was 300 miles away.

Actually, I was very excited about going away from home. I was very Happy to be graduated from high school and getting on with whatever was ahead.

Now, wouldn't you know, since I was late enrolling, the dormitories were full and I had to live "off campus". But that was ok. I was off to a new adventure! I had a new set of suitcases, "Lady Baltimore" suitcases, a large one and a "hat box". And... I had a steamer trunk.

I must tell you about my TRUNK. It was a big steamer trunk that was my Mother's. It was large, perhaps 3 cubic feet and held bedding, change of season clothes and other amazing things. Now that trunk became part of my life. It was with me through 4 years of college. It stored my clothes during PT school. It

the historical, faithful Steamer Trunk

came with me when I got married. It has stored all our out of season clothes and later the baby things. It went to school for 4 years with my daughter and came back home to my attic for more family storage. Here it stayed for many years, keeping my treasures safe. I was 17 years of age when I went off to college in 1941. And I was 89 years of age, when I finally had to say good bye to my faithful trunk. You see, because of a new air conditioner that had to be installed in my attic, mold developed and the trunk had to be destroyed. **That was a very sad day!**

The longawaited day to start my new adventure arrived. My folks drove me out to Bowling Green State University, BGSU. The day was clear and warm. We met my House Family, got me moved in and settled, and then drove to see the campus. (We had never been there before.) We liked what we saw. When it was time for my folks to head home, because the campus was on the route they would take, they just drove off from there. I was left standing on the corner waving good bye.

I will never forget how I felt as I watched them drive off. I stood there trying to remember how to get back to my lodgings. In all the excitement I never gave a thought to how we got to the campus. Poor little country girl! That is exactly what I was— young, scared, lost.

Well, I did find my way back, and I found I had 2 girls rooming across the hall from me, Mary Holt and Dorothy Wood. Mary & I became good friends for life, but Dorothy later dropped out.

That first year at BGSU was full of wonderful new experiences. We walked to & from campus, about 4 blocks as I remember. That is how I met David Harkness (more about him later).

In that year, 1941, most of the sororities on campus were local, but the National Fraternities were wooing them to become national fraternities. Mary and I were "rushed" by the local sorority, Las Amigos. That was exciting and made me feel liked and important. We joined, of course. It was a group of "nice" girls and I was one of them. The other sororities were known for drinking and smoking and other fast stuff.

When I left home, it was understood that I wouldn't get home until Christmas. Just too far and not enough time. I accepted that. After all, this was what I wanted.

But, when Thanksgiving rolled around and the school gave more time to students living 300 miles away, I was exuberant. There was no time to write my folks that I would be home, so after classes I dragged my suitcase 6 blocks to the bus station and boarded the bus. What an adventure! The bus drove south to Chillicothe, OH. where I stood outside a doorway—no bus station—waiting for the next bus to take me north and east to Red House, WVA. When I arrived there, I surprised Dad when I called him at the bank and asked him to pick me up, but don't tell Mother—let's surprise her. And that we did! It was a great home coming!

The trip back was interesting, too. My Mother made the best catsup and dill pickles. I missed them and decided to take one of each back with me. So, into the suitcase they went. The "New" suitcase was never the same again for the pickles juiced out onto everything inside. Have you ever smelled clothes wet with dill pickle juice? Never understood why my house mates wouldn't come into my room.

During the years I was at BGU, there were never any laundry facilities so we had a laundry box that we sent home about once a week. It had a lid that was secured by adjustable straps. And, on the lid was a clear plastic label that held the real the address label. It was such that the label had only to be turned over according to the destination. Very convenient! It was always a wonderful surprise to find some sort of goodie that My Dear Mother would include in the laundry box. Needless to say, I did a lot of hand washing, too.

David Harkness was a local boy living down the street from my abode. We would cross paths walking to classes. Can't remember how we became an "item" but he was around for 2 years. Then he went off to Medical school to become a dentist. We dated when he came home until one day, I decided I didn't really like him anymore and that was the end of that.

There was another boy. Can't remember his name, Dick, I think, but he got married while I was away for the summer break. I wasn't upset as some thought I would be. We were just friends.

Alpha Xi Omega Fraternity

Sorority life was good. I belonged to a sorority. I belonged!

My sophomore year our sorority moved into the 2nd floor of the Infirmary.

Housing was very limited during the war and that was the best we had. Mary and I shared a room there. Then in my Junior year we got a real house. It was the president's old home. It was a lovely old house but had limited space for all the girls needing rooms. There was a living room, dining room, a room for the House Mother, a kitchen and 2 enclosed side porches, on the first floor. One of the porches was a study room and one was the "Smoker". Yes, everyone was smoking by then—except me. I would rather spend my money on a Heath Bar.

The 2nd floor had one bathroom and 4 bedrooms. Each bedroom had two double bunks. There was little room for dressers or chestofdrawers, so the third floor was finished and the chestofdrawers were up there, as well as a 2nd toilet. Only one bath tub—and all these girls? It was very interesting.

There was one girl, who some of the gals liked to give a bad time. When she was in the bath tub they would parade through the bathroom—in one door and out the other. Not I. I didn't think it was a nice thing to do.

I remember having to make up a dance routine for one of my PE classes. I practiced a tapdancing routine on the third floor and drove everyone crazy. I did get an A.

National Fraternities were, now, wooing the local sororities. We, too, were wooed and joined The Alpha Chi Omega Fraternity in 1943. It was quite an affair, going national, with secret ceremonies and such. A lot of nonsense as far as I was concerned and was very upset when I wished to rush a very talented friend but couldn't because she was Jewish. Sadly, I was too weak to protest very much or drop out. Not that it would have done any good.

As each new year began, it was "rush" season and the incoming freshmen would be checked out for special talents & personalities good for our group. The other sororities would be interested too, so we had to really woo them. Our specialty was afternoon tea— a secret recipe for delicious spiced tea.

It's funny, but I can't seem to remember where we ate our meals, except on Sundays. Then, one of us would prepare dinner at the house. One Sunday morning Mary, the Home Economics major, woke me up and asked if I knew how to cut up a chicken. Well, I had never cut up a chicken before but had often watched my Mother do it. So, I said "sure". I have found I can bluff my way through a lot of situations. We all teased Mary, later, for the Home Economics major had to ask a Phys Ed major to help her in the kitchen.

My academic life was nothing to rave about. I passed every year with Bs & Cs. while many around me made Honor Roll every semester. Funny, as I look back, I never really knew how to study. It is amazing I did as well as I did.

The summers during those years were full. After my freshman year I was home helping with the garden and selling string beans to Smouses, the grocer in town.

WWII was raging. All the men were off fighting, leaving no one to farm the farms or work in the factories. So, the women came forward and took their places. They worked in the factories and they farmed the farms. The summers of '43 & '44 1 worked at a "Land Army Camp" helping to harvest the beans, tomatoes or to strip tobacco.

My job was to be a lifeguard, a barrack mother and work in the fields.

Women of all ages from 11 years to 67 years old would spend their vacation weeks helping to harvest the crops. They paid only for their food and received cash for each basket they picked.

picking Bean

Early each morning we would climb into the farmers truck. Can you believe, we were standing in the back of the truck? How safe was that? We would be driven to a field of string beans, or tomatoes. We would pick, filling a peck basket, which we would carry to the farmer who would give us a token for each basket. At the end of the week, we would cash in the token for money. I can't remember how much each token was worth. I kept some as a souvenir, but they got lost along the way. At the end of the day we would return to camp and swim or play ball. I was supposed to be the recreation councilor, but really, I wasn't much more than the lifeguard. We did put on a water pageant one summer. That was fun and the girls enjoyed it. I was also a barrack "Mother" for younger girls.

One day a group of us were walking up the road to a watermelon patch. The farmer caught us, but gave one of the girls a melon.

As we left the girl stumbled, dropping the melon, which broke. The farmer was kind and gave us another one. We giggled and happily carried our trophy back to camp.

I remember I would sometimes drive into Baltimore to purchase produce for the camp at the Market at the Camden Station. There was no Ritchie highway then and the Baltimore and Annapolis Road was narrow and winding.

The last summer that I worked there, before returning home, I decided to visit a friend who lived in Chestertown. We had lunch at Fisherman's Inn and I bought crabs to take home to the folks. I traveled by train (the B & O railroad) from Baltimore to Oakland. The box of crabs rode safely in a rack overhead. Everyone knew what was in it. Don't you know, there is a very distinctive smell about steamed crabs. When I got the box home and into the house, the cats were on top of it before the folks knew what was in it. A dead giveaway. Needless to say, the crabs were a great treat for everybody. It was fun!!

Who would have thought that 16 years later I would be living in a community on the Magothy River, and explore, by boat, the area where the camp used to be. On Cornfield Creek.

What was really interesting and rather funny, was, the camp was situated on Cornfield Creek off the Magothy River. The camp had

The Natatorium

been a boy's Military camp with barrack, kitchen, dining room and houses for the camp leader, nurse, assistant and cook. Ideal for a Land Army Camp. I spent those summers in the sun and when I returned to BGSU I was as black as some black people. Tans were enviable then and all my friends were jealous. At that time, we didn't know about the risk of cancer.

Back at BGSU there was Swan Club. Now, that was my passion! I would be at the Natatorium every night, practicing a routine for the pageant we would give that year. One year it was a South Sea Island theme. The finale was a sacrifice to the Gods as our, very talented, diver, dove into a ring of fire. She singed her eyebrows.

My senior year, as I was the only senior, I was president. The pageant was special that year. Remember the poem Wynken, Blynken and Nod? We had a crescent moon strung up high with three little children sitting on it, looking down as we swam formations telling of wonderful adventures. One formation was two paper mache horse's heads coming together from opposite corners of the pool. They swam in formation as if courting, then swam off together. When they emerged again two little horse's heads followed them.

swimming formation

It was really wonderful and fulfilling to be able to swim and participate in those pageants. I was never a speed swimmer, But OH, I did have form!

Our advisor was Miss Eppler, who was the head of the Physical Education department. For some reason, she liked me and suggested I do some practice

teaching as a swimming instructor there, at the college. What a deal! But, as a result, I was not ready for real practice teaching and soon discovered I would be a lousy teacher! What now? What would I do if I didn't teach?

Then one day, I went to the post office in town and saw a poster that shouted at me! THE ARMY NEEDS YOU! BECOME A PHYSICAL THERAPIST. The army will train you! Perfect! I had enjoyed the course on Care & Prevention of Athletic Injuries. I knew an alumna who was a PT. I would do it! Another new adventure ahead of me!

A few weeks before graduation I was told I was to receive a trophy. Imagine my surprise!! What was this trophy? I wasn't aware there was a trophy. After much inquiry, I learned this trophy was given to the senior girl who showed the greatest development in physical education work. Why me? I was just a swimmer. I didn't belong to any of the other sports activities or clubs. It must have been Miss Eppler's doing. She liked me. Later, I learned that one of the really active PE majors had hoped to receive that trophy. I remember her name, Lois Cochran, and she really deserved it. I have always felt a bit guilty. Really couldn't do anything about it. It was too late. My sorority had it on display until the following year when another senior PE major girl received it.

Oh gee, I've failed to tell about my bicycle. It too, has a long history. That story began back when Maurice and I were about 13 & 14. Dad said we could have a bicycle, but just one for both of us. Would it be a boy's bike or a girl's bike? Well Maurice didn't want to be seen on a girl's bike and since I was such a tom boy and didn't really care, a boy's bike it was. As I recall, I can't remember Maurice using it much. I remember only one occasion when we had a fight over it and Mother had to come and separate us.

I remember trying to ride up Court House Hill and on home without stopping. Court House Hill was about a 45° incline that rose up from Main Street, and was a block long. After reaching the top there was a gradual incline for about 6 more blocks to reach home. I began by zig zagging my way to the top, then stopping to rest. Gradually my legs got stronger and I was able to make it all the way home. The first time I accomplished that, when I got home and got off the bike, my legs were so shaky I almost fell—BUT I DID IT!! I was pretty proud that I could climb the Court House Hill and reach home without stopping.

That faithful bike was shipped out to me my junior year at BGSU. You can imagine how great it was to have wheels. No one had a car. They weren't available. The war was raging and all such manu-

facturing was for the military. We walked, unless we had a bicycle…
I was so fortunate. At the end of graduation my friend, Miss Eppler,
bought my bike for $5.00.

Chapter 3 • PT Training, Fort Custer & VA Hospital

"Go confidently in the direction of your dream
Live the life you've imagined"
—Henry David Thoreau

Life can be very frustrating at times, especially when dealing with documents on a computer. It is Thursday, September 14, 2017. After months of struggling to compose an interesting and perhaps sometime amusing account of my long life, beginning in 1924 and having gotten to the year 1989, the computer struck! I looked at a blank screen— nothing there, everything lost! I had printed the first 30 years and should have continued printing as I progressed, but such is life!

Fort Custer

It was that poster in the Post Office at BGSU, the one that yelled "Join the Army and become a Physical Therapist." that set the path for my future. First, I applied to the Air Force Hospital in Denver, CO. but it was filled; then to Warm Springs, Georgia, it too was filled. Third time is a charm, so they say, for my application to Percy Jones General Hospital in Battle Creek MI. was accepted! I'm going to join the army and become a Physical Therapist!!

On August 5, 1945 my new adventure began as I boarded the train to Battle Creek MI. It was evening when I arrived there, at the station. I had an address but no idea how to get there. I could see no form of available transportation. I was excited, I was not really scared, but I was uncertain what to do next. How do I get to the address given me? A kind army captain saw my predicament and my uncertainty and offered to share a taxi, then directed me to The Battle Creek Sanitarium, where I spent the night. It was the starting point for my enlistment. The next morning, I walked across the street to the hospital where I was to check in.

First impressions can be indelible in one's brain, for as I walked into the building and down a long hall looking for the office, all of a sudden, out of an elevator came a patient in a wheel chair. He came flying out and soared down the hall—a nurse in close pursuit— the patient yelling "look out you two legged people!" Goodness!

I continued walking and I passed another patient dressed in hospital pajamas and robe. He had no face! I admit, I was taken aback. He was a pilot whose plane had been hit and caught fire. He was badly burned.

I have no recollection of finding the office or of signing in, or of the bus that took me to my living quarters on the Fort Custer Army Post. The bus deposited me at an army barracks where I found my room. We each had our separate room. There was one bathroom down the hall, with toilet stalls and one tub—no showers. We were really quite comfortable with an army cot, dresser and a table where we could study. Classes were held in a separate barracks. We ate with the officers, (no mingling with enlisted personnel) in their mess hall.

The first 6 months was intense studying of anatomy, physiology, physics, physical therapy methods; such as massage, use of heat lamps and diathermy, etc. There wasn't much time for play. We had army lieutenants and captains as instructors. I remember one Captain in particular (but not his name). He was trying to teach us physics which was important in understanding the electrical equipment we would be using. Class was at one o'clock, right after lunch. It was summer; it was hot, no air conditioning. We couldn't keep our eyes open. He would be showing diagrams on a screen so the windows were covered. I guess he understood our problem, for when he saw a head nod, he would tap the shoulder with his pointer stick.

In February, after 6 months of heavy duty studying and testing, we received our "beautiful" uniforms and were capped. The dress was royal blue with separate, heavily starched white collar and cuffs, all of which had to be pinned on every morning. The dress hung straight with 2 tucks at each shoulder and a belt to cinch in the waist which had to be pinned also. (We needed 8 pins to complete the ensemble.)

The dress could be no shorter than 1 inch below the patella (the knee cap) so we stood and were measured. The cap was a cute little white starched "nurses" hat. The uniforms were provided and laundered for us.

There was a ceremony! Each student had a sponsor who did the honors of placing the caps on our heads. The sponsors were our instructors or women involved with the school in some way. My sponsor was a Mrs. Stevens. Of course, pictures were taken.

We were all excited and apprehensive when we began our first day of practical application. There were 3 areas in which we had to work. Percy Jones General Hospital in Battle Creek, the Annex, and Rehab on the Fort.

The patients at the hospital were mostly bed patients and needed exercises adapted to lying in bed—passive and assistive exercises to maintain joint motion and muscle strength. There was one patient that is still so vivid in my mind. He was lying on a Stryker Frame (a sort of hammocklike frame that can be flipped over so the patient can be on his back or on his stomach. Thus, preventing bed sores.). He had been a general in the Pacific and a Japanese POW. He had been tortured. He looked like a skeleton with skin. Our job was to move his arms and legs through passive ranges of motion. It was very painful for him. I have often wondered if he ever recovered.

The Annex was a step closer to patient discharge. There the patients were walking with canes or on crutches. They were mostly amputees, or men with peripheral nerve injuries (injuries of the nerves in the extremities resulting in some paralysis in the arms and hands or legs and feet). Peripheral nerves can usually regenerate. The muscle needs to be stimulated to prevent atrophy while the regeneration takes place. We used electrical stimulation to contract the muscles and then had the patient concentrate on moving that particular muscle.

I remember one patient— (a goodlooking man!?!) He was sitting on a plinth with his right leg (the one we were working on) stretched out but the left was hanging over the side. The nerves were regenerating in the lower leg and we were working on the ankle and toes. When I asked him to pull his toes up; then down, then spread

hitcho Driking to Port Huron

them apart, he laughed. I said "you can do it with the other foot". He really laughed then and lifted his left leg up onto the plinth—it was an artificial leg! Guess who had a red face?

The third area was on the post and was the last step to discharge "the rehab area". It was heavy duty exercises and some sports, but I never did duty there.

Life was not all work and study. That first Labor Day we had an extra day off. What to do so far from home. Another student friend, Sully (we all went by our last names, hers was Sullivan), had a friend who owned a cottage at Port Huron, on Lake Huron, across the state from Battle Creek. Sully wanted to spend the holiday there. Would I consider hitchhiking with her across the state? Of course, I would! So, we set out after work, on Friday afternoon. No problem. Our first ride was with two of Sully's patients. I don't recall their names, but the driver was wearing an Airplane Splint (a brace that holds the arm, with elbow bent, out at a right angle, from the body) on his right arm but his left arm and legs were good. He could work the pedals and steer the car but could not shift the gears. His copilot wore 2 long leg braces but his arms were good so he could shift the gears. We were good to go and rode with them about half way. They needed to head north, we were going east, so we took our leave and started thumbing again. We turned down one offer. We didn't like the looks of him but without much waiting we were on our way again. It was uneventful and we arrived in Port Huron safely. It is funny the things one remembers and the things one does not remember. I have no recollection of what we did while at the cottage. I just remember Sully had a friend who drove us back to Fort Custer.

Carmella (another student) had a car! One Sunday we drove up to Holland Michigan to see the Tulip Festival. It was so beautiful with so many different colors of tulips everywhere one looked throughout the town, over acres and acres of fields. We could see people walking out in the fields, selecting the bulbs they wanted to buy. I guess they ordered them and had them sent in time for fall planting.

One evening Carmella offered to drive a car load of us to an Aquatic Show at Michigan State University. Peg Knott, a graduate from there, had suggested we go see it. I especially wanted to go for I had taken part in such shows at Bowling Green. The show was fun! The trip home was even more fun. We stopped at a roadside eatery where we teamed up with a car load of our patients. I only remember the driver of their car, Cpl Ervin Lang. We happened to be sitting next to each other. He was funny. He seemed to like me. What did we talk about? I don't remember. I just remember how much fun it was!

The following Monday morning I began my duties at the Annex.

Ern & canoeing on Eagle Lake

To my surprise, the first patient to walk through the door was none other than this Cpl Ervin Lang. He was laughing, joking, teasing and giving the aids a hard time. His good humor was not appreciated by those suffering from the "morning after blues". Yes, here was my friend of the roadside eatery, Cpl Ervin Lang, and he was on my schedule.

Cpl Lang had received a gunshot wound in his left upper leg, severing the femoral artery and fracturing the femur. Fortunately, there was no nerve damage but the circulation into the left lower extremity was greatly compromised. The body has marvelous powers of recovery. It has a remarkable system of collateral circulation which would supply most of the leg. However, the toes were too far away from the source of the blood supply and gangrene had set into his toes. They had to be amputated. The fractured femur had to be put into a cast and up in a sling, resulting in a deep callus forming on the back of the heel. The fracture had healed so Lang was at the Annex being rehabilitated toward discharge. My job, as his PT, was to try and improve the mobility of the left ankle. As a result of the trauma and being immobilized in a cast for so long the ankle had frozen. Also, he had to learn to walk with artificial toes in his shoe. Surprising how important the toes are.

That was the beginning of a fine romance! If someone were to ask me, now, what was the happiest time of my life, I would not hesitate to say, "that time in late July and early August of the year 1946". There were only a few days before I would graduate from PT School. But, we made the most of them.

Just imagine…it was summer. We didn't have a care in the world. We had no responsibilities. We were fed, clothed, and had a roof over our heads. My hours were from 8 to 4 with Saturday afternoon and Sunday off!! There was a small Lake, Eagle Lake, down the hill from the Annex, an ideal spot to meet after a day's work. We would swim, soak up the sun and talk, getting to know each other.

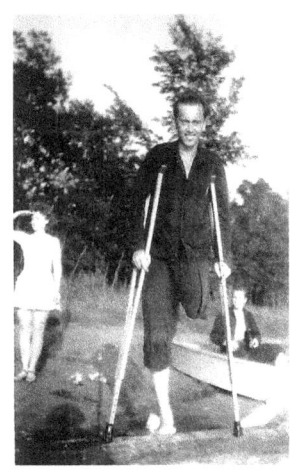

He had a car so we ended the day by going out for a hamburger or something, maybe a movie until curfew. We visited the Kellogg Bird Sanctuary. We went horseback riding with another couple, Esther Lanto and Hoppy Hopkins.

Now that was another adventure! Hoppy was an above knee amputee, wearing a prosthesis. He was a farm boy who claimed he knew all about riding horses. We mounted up (Hoppy needing some help, having only one leg) and set out, with Hoppy leading at a good clip. As we

33

rounded a turn in the trail, I saw Hoppy slip off his horse. The turn was against his prosthesis, there was no leg to help him cling to the horse so he rolled off. I watched him roll under the horse as it went on. Then I saw Hoppy nonchalantly pick himself up, brush himself off, take a comb from his pocket and comb his hair. Down the path the horse was waiting for him, but how was he going to remount with only one leg? Fortunately, there was a rail fence along the trail and he was able to lead the horse to it and climb up on one of the rails, and throw his prosthesis over the horse. We were on our way again. August 14 soon arrived, when we were to graduate and join the army as a 2nd Lieutenant for the duration and 6 months. The duration was over, the war had ended on August 1945 this was 1946. I believe we were the last class to be government trained. There didn't seem to be the same need for Physical Therapists so we were given a choice—we could commit to the army or we could choose to stay civilian.

My friend, May Mosser, had been dating one of the soldiers who was working in the Rehab Center. He was being discharged and going home to Chicago to finish school and then join his father's business. Mary wanted to follow him and needed someone to share room, etc. Then she told me she had talked with Erv who said he would have nothing to do with a WAAC and if I stayed with the army, he would end our relationship. Now, I never heard it from him but that was OK. I took the job at the VA hospital. (I guess I thought I was paying back the government by working there.) It wasn't far from Battle Creek where Erv was still a patient. He had a car and could come visit me.

So, it was—I moved to Berwyn IL, which was near the hospital, with my friend Mary. We rented a single room in a boarding house for $60 a month. We shared a bath with another couple and had an outside stair. No cooking facilities and no telephone. Mary had her car, VAGA, (named

for the Vagus nerve (it increases heart palpitations) which was our transportation to & from work.

There was a problem, tho, Mary was off every evening & weekend day, spending time with Don at his school library, leaving me alone. I was afraid to take a bus anywhere. Not being a city girl, standing on a street corner waiting for a bus didn't seem like a good idea.

When the Christmas Holidays arrived, I flew home. I told my folks how lonely I was for I couldn't get out; I had no transportation and was afraid to take a bus. Well you know, this was right after the war. The car manufacturers had not caught up on making domestic vehicles. There were few cars to be had. My wonderful Dad took pity on me and sold me his car for $600. He was sure the car he had on order would be in soon. It wasn't until much later that I learned he had walked to work for several months (the sacrifices a Dad will make for his daughter).

Mary in my new Chevrolet

The morning was cold and with a slight rain when I headed back. (I was going to Cleveland first, to meet up with Erv, for he was on leave before discharge.) I couldn't sleep, so was up at 4 and on the road early. This was December. There was a heater under the dash board in the car, but no defroster, so a tiny fan on the steering shaft blew hot air onto the windshield.

As I headed north to the Pennsylvania Turnpike, I am happy as a lark. I had a new car and was going to see Erv! That is, until I realized the wheels were not getting traction on the road. The rain was freezing. As I came to a curve and a downhill grade. I veered to the shoulder thinking there would be better traction. I noticed a car with chains pushing another car up the hill in the other direction. Just then my car spun around, across the road and landed with the back end against the bank, just where a big stump was protruding. All I could think of was, "Oh my new car! my new car!" I got out to investigate the damage. The stump was embedded in the trunk. I was so unnerved that when the car that I had seen going up came back & offered me a lift into the town I took him up on it. The garage man there drove me back to my car. It was a great relief to learn only the trunk was damaged. The engine was at the other end— what a blessing!! I was able to continue on my way.

First stop was Cleveland to see Erv and meet his family for the first time. I was very warmly received, though Erv's mother was horrified that I would drive all that way by myself. His family consisted of Mom (Bertha), Dad, (Carl), sisters Alma (16), & Lillian (14).

Now, a very ridiculous situation developed that I didn't seem to have any control over. Erv didn't want me to drive on to Berwyn alone (for goodness sakes, I had already driven 400 miles, alone). He insisted I fly back to Berwyn, then in a week when his leave was over, I would fly back to Cleveland and we would drive back in tandem. I can't remember if he drove all the way to Berwyn with me and then back to Battle Creek, but I guess he did. Wasn't that really silly!? He was already taking charge of my life.

Now that I had transportation, I could go places. Mother & Dad had friends who lived in Oak Park, nearby. They invited me to their home for dinner and to see this new thing called television. He worked for RCA and was promoting Television. It was a black and white with an 8inch screen. We watched wrestling. The idea of seeing a TV before they were even in the stores was exciting, but can't say much for the wrestling.

Back at work at Hines, Mary & I decided it was foolish to live in Berwyn and drive to the hospital everyday when it was possible to live on the Hospital Campus at no charge other than food. So, we moved into the barrack there. I don't remember how many PT's and nurses lived there. We had cots separated by tall metal wardrobes and a sort of table. Foot lockers at the foot of the cot. It was really quite OK. It was convenient to work, we were fed and had a roof over our heads and I had company. What more could a working girl trying to pay for a new car ask?

Work at the VA was interesting. There were several different units in the PT department. Mary was with the Respiratory unit and I was with the Rehab unit where patients who were suffering from strokes, or Multiple Sclerosis or Muscular Dystrophy, etc, would receive treatment. My job was to try and relieve any pain, keep the joints and muscles flexible and possibly reeducate the muscles.

There are 2 stories I want to tell. We had one very sweet gentleman who had had a stroke and had lost his ability to verbally connect. He had aphasia. Each morning an aide would wheel him down for PT. We would welcome him with, "Good Morning Mr. Becker!!" With a very broad grin and a twinkle in his eye he would always respond with, "son of a bitch, son of a bitch." You see, those were the only words that would come out. It is sad but he was happy to see us and we were happy to see him.

We also had patients from the psychiatric ward who had received shock treatment. They were sore and achy from the convulsion caused by the shock treatments, so, we would place a large infra red lamp over them for about 20 minutes to relax the muscles.

One noon, as we returned from lunch, we found one of these patients sitting on a bench in the hall, as though waiting for treatment. We had a male PT working with us, who wore a white coat, like the men who gave the shock treatments. The patient sitting in the hall associated the two and proceeded to attack the PT. Across the hall were 3 "heavy duty exercise" fellows. They came to the rescue. They were able to grab the patient and hold him until someone arrived with a strait jacket. Then the patient was escorted back to his ward.

That male PT will probably expand on that story for years to come. (A male PT was an oddity back then. Like nursing, PT was a female profession.)

When his leave ended, Erv returned to the hospital, looking forward to discharge. This was not to happen. The callus on the heel was draining. Gangrene had set in and the leg needed to be amputated. Fortunately, the leg above the knee was healthy and the amputation would be below the knee. (Guess there is always something to be grateful for.)

During the month or so of his recovery and before he was able to walk with a prosthesis, I would spend every weekend with him. After a half day of work on Saturday, Mary would drive me to the train station where I would catch the train to Battle Creek. Sometimes I rode the elevated to the train station, but wasn't really happy doing so. I didn't like riding high on just rails. It frightened me (What we do for LOVE).

It would be late afternoon when the train reached Battle Creek. I would walk to the hotel, check in then go visit Erv.

One trip, after I had gathered my belongings, stepped off the train, and was heading up to the hotel I looked down the street and saw a man sort of running—HE WAS NAKED! I didn't pause but took off as fast as I could to the hotel. Goodness!

One weekend when I was scheduled to go see Erv, I was very sick with the flu with a 104 temperature. I was in bed and unable to go. I remember the nurse coming; I remember having a lot of soup brought to me;

Mary sent a telegram to Erv, saying I was too sick to come, and signed my name. He wondered if I was so sick how could I get to Berwyn to send the telegram. Well! I quickly took care of that misunderstanding.

Again, I don't remember exact dates, but as soon as Erv felt confident with his prosthesis, he began driving to Hines on weekends. His Dad, a real genius with machinery, had fixed the car so Erv could drive without using the clutch. Our barrack had no "lounge" for entertaining so I would have to meet him at the door and then we would go out: to a movie, to eat or to just neck (of course, we did).

One evening we found a side road and were parked when there was a tap on the window. We were startled and a bit worried, were we safe? But it was a policeman who was very nice and suggested we leave. He said it was not safe where we were, however, there was a park that was lit and we could go there. When we arrived at the park we had to laugh. It seems that park was a favorite spot, for there were a lot of other cars parked there, too.

Again, exact dates elude me, but Erv was finally discharged. He went home to Cleveland where his old job was waiting for him in the personnel office of Columbia Axel Co. His Dad and Dick Sopko were also working there.

The Government was good to veterans, back then. Upon his discharge, the government issued him a brandnew car. An Oldsmobile. It was specially equipped with "fluid drive"— no clutch. This enabled the amputee to drive without having to use the left leg. Neat, uh? And it was RED!

Chapter 4 • 1947, Cleveland

"People grow through experience if they meet
life honestly and courageously."
—Eleanor Roosevelt

Erv and I corresponded regularly, but really wanted to be together. Finally, in May, I left Hines VA Hospital and moved to Cleveland. Erv had arranged for me to stay with his Aunt & Uncle, Tanta and Uncle Taufenbach. I would just room with them, but take meals out.

My first introduction to the Lang Clan was the first Sunday I arrived. His sister Lillian was celebrating her confirmation. Big party! I was told not to worry about names for if the person was my age just call them "cousin" and if they were older call them "Tanta" or "Uncle" That was easy. There were many in the Lang Clan and I was glad the names were made simple. The one thing I do remember is taking off my shoes and dancing the polka with everyone. I had a wonderful time!

My new job was at the prestigious Cleveland Clinic, on Prospect Ave in downtown Cleveland. My hours were 8 AM to 5 PM; an hour for lunch and half day on Saturday. I seldom ate breakfast but had lunch at the Clinic and found a neat restaurant that was on my way home. They served a delicious Western Omelet.

During the summer months, when roses were in bloom, and before he would go to work, Uncle, who was so proud of his roses, would put a rose in a glass and set it with a glass of orange juice on the table for me every morning. They liked me and I was spoiled. I really liked them, too.

About my job at the Cleveland Clinic: my boss was a Miss Witterhaus. She was the director of their Physical Therapy School as well as head of their Physical Therapy Department. She was a commanding figure—we were all a bit afraid of her and when she said "jump!" we jumped. When summer days became so hot, (no air conditioning), she would say, "think cool" and put fans on shelves up high to circulate the air. I began by working in the clinic but then moved to treating patients on the floors. It meant moving the heat lamps and ultra violet machines on & off elevators to the patient's rooms. I was on call. After we married, I loved hearing, **"Paging Mrs. Lang".**

Erv was living with his family about an hour away, but he would drive over every evening to be with me. He made sure I was not lonely. We were together every weekend, spending time with his family, dining out with some of his old friends or going to a movie or whatever.

Then, one evening (it just happened to be August first, my birthday) Tanta & Uncle were away and Erv's cousin Alice was chaperoning me. She suggested I do my nails and dress up special. Erv arrived and, for my birthday, gave me a wonderful portable radio.

And an absolutely gorgeous diamond ring. A large center diamond with 3 smaller settings on each side. We were officially engaged!!! We took pictures of my left hand with the sparkles on the third finger.

The wedding would not be for another year, for Erv wanted a big German Wedding & Reception, with a rented hall, polka band, sit down dinner and lots of food and beer. One needed to reserve the hall a year ahead, so we set the date for Saturday June 26, 1948. (It just happened to be Erv's Mom & Dad's wedding anniversary. How about that?)

It was exciting, anticipating MY wedding. I really was a country bumpkin! I had absolutely no idea how to go about planning a wedding. I had never been to a wedding. I don't know if there were even wedding magazines back then. Fortunately, Erv knew what he wanted and took care of all the details, but with my help making final decisions. But I did need to buy a trousseau. Being a new kid in town and not being much of a "shopper" I didn't know the stores or how to find them. That was when Alice took me in hand and helped me find the necessary items for my trousseau. The dress was a lovely satin with long sleeves and a sweetheart neckline and a hoop, which I hoped would not flip up when I knelt at the altar. The hoop had fancy lace with bows and flowers around the bottom that showed where the dress was pulled up at intervals around the hem. The veil was shoulder length with a tiara. I was the cat's meow! My shoes were satin with really high heels. No, fortunately, I didn't fall flat on my face.

We were married in Erv's family's church. Zion Lutheran Church was the oldest Lutheran church in Cleveland. It had two services, one service was conducted in German which Erv's family attended. They were very active there with Dad being on council and Erv attending the grade school.

There were 12 in our wedding party. Imagine! There were just a lot of people whom we needed to include. There was Alice, my matron of honor; then Alma, Helen Kendel, and Edna Stewart as my bridesmaids with Charlotte and Lillian as flower girls.

Erv's attendants were my brother Maurice as best man, and Freddie Kendel, Howard Williams and Elmer Stewart as his groomsmen.

Dressing at Tanta's, getting to the church—it's all a bit of a haze. The ceremony is more of a haze and walking back down the aisle as Mrs. Ervin Lang is a haze too. Fortunately, we have photographs of it all to help me remember just what it was all about. The photo of our walking back down the aisle shows both of us grinning from ear to ear. We did it!

What a wonderful time was had by all! Though Erv & I left at midnight, we were told later that the party lasted until 4 in the morning. My good Methodist parents had never experienced such an affair!!

We spent the night at a hotel in downtown Cleveland and caught an early boat across the lake to Toronto, Canada. Our destination was north to Windermere on

Lake Rousseau. It rained as we drove north, arriving there in the evening. We must have looked very bedraggled for when we came down the next morning, they didn't recognize us.

A honeymoon isn't all it's said to be, especially if the bride has her "period" One just can't plan that far ahead of time. Poor Erv!

The days were good. We spent a week there, driving around, seeing the sights— my first sight of river locks. We bought a beautiful maroon colored Hudson Bay blanket.

Erv had brought along a 2 hp outboard motor so we rented a boat and went out on the lake to do some swimming.

There was another couple on their honeymoon, too, and they joined us. We found a spot with some rocks and bushes where Erv could go and remove his leg. He was very sensitive about that and thought we were laughing at him. How wrong! But the fun was spoiled.

We were looking forward to stopping at Niagara Fall on the way home. Remember this is June and it's hot and no air conditioning. We had a room in a hotel that looked out onto the Falls or so we were told. Our room was in the back and no Falls were visible. However, we settled in for the night, but it was so terribly hot we got up at 4 in the morning and drove home.

I discovered I liked very much being married to Cpl Ervin C. Lang. His family took me in with open arms and there were a lot of arms! There was "Old" Tanta & Uncle Lang in Footville, with four sons. I can't remember the name of the oldest, but there was Wally, Erwin. & Harold. (Harold had brought home an English war bride named Ellen). There was Uncle Eddie and Tanta Tillie Gerlat who had a farm near Footville. They had 2 sons, Norman and Leonard. There was Tanta Albina, & Uncle Kokosky & Edwin; There was the Fedroviches, and more.

Our first home was a 2room apartment over Erv's folk's garage. It was really quite nice for a starter. A large front room/bedroom, a kitchen & bath. I look back and remember how very hot it was that first year. Of course, there was no air conditioning. We pulled our mattress over to the window, set a pan of ice cubes on a stand and a fan in the win-  dow. It would blow across the ice and cool us. I was almost sick from the heat and working with heat at the Clinic. I had to take off a few days. (Trying to be a good wife and working too…)

 In 1949 we moved to a 2nd floor 2bedroom apartment at 12408 Maple Ave, a stone's throw from the Kendel's. I remember, we had gotten a red plastic silverware holder for a wedding gift, and our landlord who lived on the first floor under us, complained about the noise it made when we dropped the silver into it. (sorry about that!)

Cleveland had a record snow that winter. Nothing was moving, shops and schools were closed. Army trucks and tanks helped take people to hospitals. Milk was $1 a quart. Folks were outraged. We enjoyed it! Erv put chains on the car and we and the Kendels headed down-town to see a movie—I believe it was Quo Vadis.

By 1950 I had changed jobs and was working at Huron Road  Hospital. Erv, too, had changed jobs and was working at US Air Compressor along with his Dad and Dick Sopko. Erv was working a lot of overtime and I was buying "war bonds" with each pay check. We saved and were soon able to purchase a small 4 ½ room bungalow at 3861 East 186th St in south east Cleveland. The price was $1200. Using a VA loan, we could make it. It was a new house in a new development of homes much like it. There was a front room, kitchen/kitchenette, 2 bedrooms and a bath, an unfinished attic and a basement. We were able to choose our own colors. We later finished the attic for Ricky's very own room. There was a garage. I believe the lot was 50' x 75'. We were happily ensconced and ready for a family.

Not sure why, but I had changed jobs again and was working in the Polio Division of Cleveland City Hospital. There was no vaccine for Polio then and it was a devastating disease. Sometimes the nerves would regenerate and we would try to teach the muscle to work again. There were hot compresses, a lot of stretching (sometimes very painful), massaging and then muscle reeducation and strengthening exercises. There was the "Iron Lung" too, for patients whose breathing muscles were paralyzed. One of those patients became a friend and we corresponded until she died. She was able to breathe again on her own but never regained enough muscle power to live without help. She was in a nursing home all her life. I found it amazing that she was always cheerful.

The Salk Vaccine became available in 1955.

Cleveland was where Erv grew up, went to school, went to church. He still had those friends from "back when" they all were members of Zion Luther Church. Friendships deeply rooted. There were Freddie and Helen Kendel, Ann & Ernie Urbus, Eddie and Norma Miller, and Ethel and Bill Petro. Bless them all—they liked me!

I am having trouble remembering about the social events with those friends. There were dinners out, parties at the Kendel's, movies, and special parties at the cottage. I do remember one Christmas party. We were in our new home. It was a Christmas Tree trimming party. Ethel got drunk and fell into the tree while holding an ornament in her hand, cutting her hand. We had to take her to the emergency room to have it sewed up. There was always a lot of drinking and that distressed me.

Chapter 5 • The Cottage

"Happiness is not something readymade. It comes from your own actions."
—Buddha saying

That fall of '48 we bought property on the Grand River, south of Geneva On the Lake, near Footville, about 50 miles away. We partnered with Bill and Ethel Petro, and together we had 300 feet of river frontage. The process of clearing the land and building a cottage was quite an exciting adventure. Especially for the Guys! As soon as the snows were gone, every Saturday, Erv, Dad Lang, Bill and the Cousins would head to the cottage to clear the land. I would pack a lunch for them. I remember the canned hams I would buy for their lunches. One doesn't see canned hams anymore.

The Guys really enjoyed this adventure. They returned home, after one trip, telling about pulling the heavy grape vines out of the trees. Cousin Edwin would climb the tree and attach a rope to the grape vine, then the other end would be tied to the back of the Plymouth coupe. The coupe would drive away and pull the vine down out of the tree. However, occasionally, the vine would be so strong it would lift up the back of the car. I can well imagine the shouting and laughter.

The cottage was a prefab brought in on a big flatbed truck. There were walls, partitions and a roof on it, but, I think, that was all.

Erv's family had a wonderful friend, Tony, who had been a carpenter. He enjoyed being a part of the family and was there every weekend working with them. When the screened in porch was added he made the scalloped trim over the porch and built little stools for Ricky and Laurie. The end product was a fine little cottage with 3 rooms and a very small bath (one you walked in and backed out or backed in and walked out). Until the septic tank was put in, we used a great big ole tree near the woods.

I had such fun making curtains and slipcovers and painting Pennsylvania Dutch designs on the wooden furniture. The bookcase was made of bricks and wood planks. Two stacked bricks at each end and a plank for the shelf. There were two shelves—it worked fine!

We brought drinking water from home, but there was a well with a hand pump near our lot where water was available for washing and we would boil it to do dishes.

Once the cottage was raised and furnished, a dock was built for easy access to the boat. Of course, there was a boat! Erv and his Dad built it! They bought a kit and, in the garage, below our apartment, they put it together. I could hear them arguing, and could hear Dad say "the directions don't know what they're talking about."

It was a sturdy 14 footer with a red stripe. I painted a mermaid on the bow. We loved to ride up and down the river! And it was fun exploring the River. It was a narrow river. A good arm could throw a stone across it. The river banks were several feet high and mucky. No sandy beaches except across from our cottage where there was a very small sand bar. We would swim there or we would just swim off the boat.

One summer my folks came out and my Dad built us an outdoor fireplace. That was the crowning touch! There is nothing quite like a quiet evening, eating Sloppy Joes around an open fire.

The Kendels and Erv and I can attest to that. It wasn't until the next morning that we discovered the Sloppy Joes were full of mosquitoes. But who cared?

One fall, Erv invited his buddies from work to a Clam Bake (can't recall their names). One man arrived early to set up. A fire was built in the fireplace, a grate across with a big tall pot on top. Inside the pot was water, then, layered chicken, sweet potatoes, veggies and clams done up in mesh bags. As they all cooked, juices from each dripped down into the water making a clam broth which was sooo delicious! It was a really cold day and some of the men even wore babushkas. The beer flowed and everyone had a grand time!

The cottage became a favorite weekend retreat for us and for family and friends. The Kendels were the most frequent visitors, bringing Stevie and Linda to enjoy the boating and swimming.

Dick Sopko was Erv's longtime friend. They had worked together at Colombia Axel and now at US Air Compressor. They were Best Buddies. We didn't see them often for they were having babies (being good Catholics) but on occasion, Dick would bring Vi and the children to the cottage. One year they vacationed for a week at the cottage. There was always joking and laughter when Dick and Erv were together. They were my favorite of the "friends."

When Ethel and Bill divorced, we bought their lots on the river. We now had all 300 feet of water frontage—neat!

Early one spring, after an especially cold winter, we rode out to the cottage to see if everything was ok. We were there just in time to hear a roaring sound from up the river. We stood on the bank awed, as we watched an "Ice Flow". Huge, I mean huge! thick slabs of ice were pushing and rearing up, then crashing down on each other, climbing the banks, leaving some there then rushing on down the river. It lasted only a few minutes, but what an amazing experience! I can

still hear the roar and see the ice as it rushed by. The wonders of Mother Nature!

In 1958 the Grand River flooded. The dam below us was blocked by fallen trees. The water rose to cover the pier, into the house and over the stove. What a mess!! Mud was thick on the floors. The linoleum had to be replaced. The books were all ruined. The veneer came off my painted furniture. I was so sad. It took buckets and buckets of water to clean the floors. Somehow it wasn't fun anymore. We moved in 1960 and there was a second flood before we could sell it. We were sorry that Mom & Dad had to do the cleaning up, this time, for we weren't there.

Chapter 6 • Starting a Family

"Courage is resistance to fear. Mastery of fear.
Not absence of fear."
—Mark Twain

I quit work in early 1952 and soon became pregnant—guess work kept me too tired. It was wonderful, being pregnant! I would tell others that if I could always feel this good, I wouldn't mind being pregnant all the time. Since this was before sonograms, we didn't know if this baby would be a boy or a girl, but ??? was a strong kicker and all out front. Some said that indicated a boy. Little did they know how true was their prediction.

Very early on the morning of November 11, 1952 we were on our way to the hospital. (It was about an hour away.) Then the contractions stopped. I felt so silly and didn't want to go there if it was a false alarm. Erv's folks lived only a few blocks from the hospital so we woke them all up and we all sat around the kitchen table waiting for the contraction to start again. The family, especially Alma and Lillian, were beside themselves with excitement! They would soon be Aunts and Mom and Dad would have their first grandchild.

Around midmorning the contractions started again and we were off to the hospital. For real, this time. The nurses said I would be in labor at least until late afternoon. I wasn't about to wait that long so they all came rushing in a little later when the water broke. It wasn't so much fun after that. I remember the terrible need to push—like dry heaves (I guess I was partially knocked out). When I came to, Erv was by my side. He proudly informed me we had a baby boy, who's ears, his father was quick to say, were tiny, like his. We had a son!—Richard Ervin Lang! Born November 12, 1952.

This was the era when we were kept in the hospital for a week. When I went home my Mother came to be with me. After all, a woman needed her Mother at a time like this. We were so pampered back then.

It was a happy time—a good life with a happy little son (once we realized he was hungry and fed him more than just formula). When he was about 4 months old and able to sit up and look around, I would set him in the bassinet and roll him wherever I would be. I remember when I was painting vegetables on the drop ceiling of the kitchen, Ricky would be in the bassinet playing and watching me and keeping me company. We were both content being together.

We continued going to the cottage where Erv was always happy and busy working around the place. As soon as Ricky began walking, he was following at the heels of his Dad who didn't mind at all. Father and son working together.

On holidays, when the family would get together, the Aunts would delight in sitting and reading to their favorite nephew. They didn't dare miss reading a page or he would remind them. On occasion, when we wanted a night out, we would take him to Nany and Papa who were always happy to babysit. I can't help it, but I just have to say it: Ricky was the cutest and happiest and 'goodest' little boy there ever was!! So there! He was never a problem! Honest.

Life was good. Erv was working a lot of over time. We were comfortably situated with our own home—a happy family with 2 cars in the driveway, a summer cottage and lots of Lang relatives for big social events. There were friends too. The Kendels continued to spend a lot of time with us, particularly on Saturday evening and every summer weekend at the cottage. (Here, I have to admit, I was not always happy that they had made themselves so much a part of our life.)

I need to tell you about Freddie & Helen Kendel for they were very much a part of our life, even after we moved to Maryland. I never really liked Freddie, but tolerated him, but I thought a lot of Helen. Freddie and Helen, especially Helen, had been very good friends of Erv's even before he went into the Army. After he was injured and

was home at Crile Military Hospital in Cleveland, Helen would regularly visit him. He was forever grateful and never forgot how she would have to take a street car across town even though she was pregnant with Stevie. When we were married, she and Freddie were in the wedding

Freddie & Helen Kendel, Stevie, and Linda

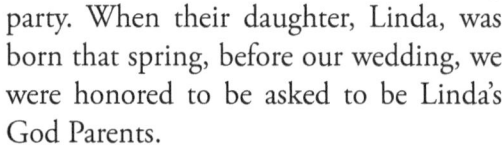

party. When their daughter, Linda, was born that spring, before our wedding, we were honored to be asked to be Linda's God Parents.

Stevie must have been 8 or 9 when he was diagnosed with leukemia. That was a very dark cloud that had fallen over that family. They were devastated! Freddie's mother & sister lived with them and they catered to Freddie's every whim. His grief for Stevie's illness was greater than anyone else and he needed to be comforted more than anyone else. Often of an evening, Freddie's sister, Wilma, would call up Erv, "would you please come and comfort Freddie?" We lived south and they lived north, but distance was of no consequence when a friend was in need. Erv was always willing to go sit with Freddie. Erv was like that!

Stevie loved to be at the Cottage. So, Freddie would bring the family for the weekend. They had to carry Stevie for he was so ill. I don't remember how long he lived with the disease. He died in November for I remember how they put up and decorated a tree on his grave at Christmas.

Trip back home

Erv's sisters were so young when I first met them. I remember the first time I saw them. Lillian asked if I would like to play "Pickup". I loved games, so said "yes". She proceeded to throw a deck of cards on the floor and said "pick up". Some initiation into the family!

Now, she is grown up, out of high school, working, and getting married. June 7, 1954 Lillian joined hands in holy matrimony with David Brueggemann. This, too, was a big German wedding. They took up residence in Bay Village, west of Cleveland, situated on the shores of Lake Erie. They built a lovely house there, within walking distance of the Lake. One could walk to the Park on the lake where one could swim and fish or just enjoy the view. It was a nice walk which Lillian and I often did, when we visited them.

Now, I did miss my family. My brother, Maurice, had done his stint in the army and was home in Salisbury MD, being a Civil Engineer, building roads and bridges. He had married Miriam the April before my wedding in June. There was little sister, Charlotte, 10 years my junior, and a rascal brother, Norman, 14 years younger. I missed them!

We would travel east to Salisbury, MD one year and my folks would come out to Cleveland the next year. The trip was about 450 miles, taking about 9 hours. We would travel early morning or late afternoon—hoping the children would sleep. We devised numerous plans for the back seat such as putting the crib mattress back there so Ricky could stretch out and sleep or play. There were no child car seats or even seat belts. We would stop at the Turnpike Plazas to have a bite to eat, relieve ourselves and walk about.

Erv was an excellent driver. He drove fast and concentrated on the road & the other drivers. But—he hated to make frequent stops. I remember one stop when I needed to 'go'. His comment was "now I have to pass all those trucks again".

The Penn Turnpike made the trip easier. However, when we came to the Chesapeake Bay, there was no bridge and we often had a long wait for the ferry boat. It was fun, tho, riding the Ferry Boat.

In June 1955 my sister, Charlotte, married Charles Wheatley. I was so proud to be asked to be my little sister's Matron of Honor. Ricky and I flew to Washington, then caught a plane to Salisbury. Ricky was only 2½. He was a trooper. It was an easy trip. I have a picture of him at the airport.

The wedding was lovely. My Dad had grown special lilies for the church decorations and Mother served an elegant rehearsal dinner, with all her best dishes, silver, lovely center pieces, the best of everything! Even though it rained that day, the wedding was lovely, the bride beautiful and all went well.

Ricky and I flew back home where Erv eagerly awaited us. We missed each other! And, so, we made another baby.

It was March 11, 1956 when a new member joined our family. She arrived 2 weeks earlier that expected, weighing in at 7lbs, with 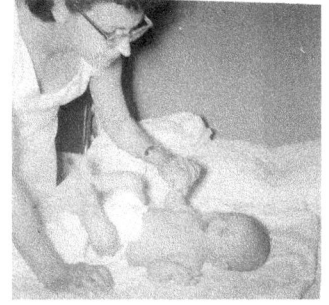 dark hair and lusty lungs. "Baby Laura Anne Lang"! (Anne was my Mother's middle name) Laurie for short.

All was not well with this little one. She had colic—another word for being in pain and no one knowing what to do to relieve that pain. So, she cried! And her Mother cried right along with her. I will never forget that time! Even now, as I recall how she would pull her little legs up and scream, I feel the agony all over again. To watch your tiny little newborn suffer! It really hurts! It is a pain worse than a physical pain.

 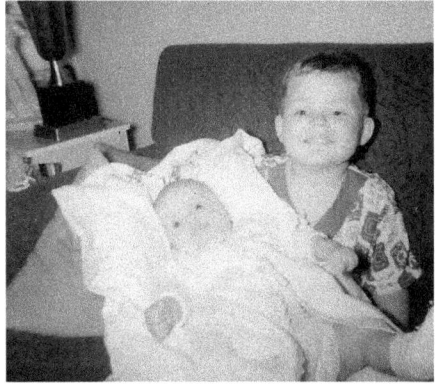

It did seem like forever, though, probably a few weeks, when we finally found a formula that agreed with her a soybean concoction. What a blessing! What a happy baby! What a happy Mommy! What a happy Daddy and little Brother. What a happy household! I am ashamed to say, I can't remember what little Brother was doing while all this was going on. He was such a good little boy and I'm sure I neglected him. "Rick, I am so sorry!"

Ricky was the pioneer. There was no one for him to watch and follow so he had to figure things out for himself—how to coordinate his legs to pedal a tricycle, how to make the fingers work to open and close scissor to cut paper. When Laurie came along, she was lucky, she had her big brother to watch and copy. It was such fun watching them learn and grow—we were delighted with them and so very proud of them! I love to look through the albums of their childhood and remember how it was.

Life was good! We continued to spend time at the cottage, weather permitting, but, with the babies we did not go during the cold weather.

The Kendels would come to visit almost every Saturday evening. Freddie's sister & mother lived with them and could baby sit Linda. Those were not such good times for me for they and Erv enjoyed their drinks (I believe it was "4 Roses" then). Inevitably the conversation would get out of hand and Freddie & Helen would argue or they would talk about sexual things that were not to my liking.

There were fun times too. There were weddings, dances with lots of food and Polka Music. I remember one dance in particular. Erv could not polka for there was little rocking motion in the artificial ankle. He hob knobbed at the bar and I sat out with his mom. She couldn't dance either because of the arthritis in her feet. We were sitting with a group of her friends who were talking together, speaking German. They were laughing about some joke when Mom turns to me, apologizing, she said," it isn't funny in English". I really had to laugh at that. She was always very kind to me. I was like another daughter and we got along very well.

When the orchestra would play a waltz, Erv and I would dance—He could dance to the slow music. I loved it when we danced—I loved having him hold me in his arms and moving together in time with the music! He really missed the dancing and he loved the polka music. He used to sing the "Blue Skirt Waltz" to me—so romantic! He had quite a collection of polka records—some old 78's, but mostly 45's and the big 33's. In later years, He enjoyed just sitting and listening to them, especially Johnny Pecon & Frankie Yankovick.

Erv's Mom and Dad were now Nany & Papa with 2 grandchildren. Then, in 19? Gary Brueggemann arrived, and 2 years later his sister, Diane.

Occasionally we would be invited to Tanta & Uncle Taufenbach's home. It was a "House Beautiful" home, immaculate, everything in place. We were always amused that we and our children would be invited but never Lillian and Dave & their children. Our Kids were well behaved!! Of course, we always took something for them to play with.

In 1959 Alma married Ray Miller They bought a very nice bungalow in Brook Park, OH. It wasn't long until they started a family. When Ray III and Glenn came along that made six grand children for Nany and Papa

In February the following year we moved to Maryland.

Chapter 7 • 1960, Move to Maryland

"The magic thing about home is that it feels good to leave, And it feels even better to come back."
—Wendy Wander

I'm not sure I mentioned that my family had moved from Oakland, to Salisbury MD in 1945. Then in 1957 they moved again to Severna Park, MD. Dad had taken the position of President of County Trust Co Bank, headquartered in Annapolis, MD. They bought a house in a waterfront community called Cape Arthur. Charlotte had married but Norman was still at home.

Erv was finding it difficult to get along with the boss where he worked and when Dad offered him a job with the bank. He was happy to accept. He began the job in December 1959 and moved in with Mother and Dad in Cape Arthur. I remained in Cleveland until the house in Cleveland was sold.

In the meantime, we bought a lot in Cape Arthur and began building a house. It's strange, I can't remember how we did it; I do remember we made several trips to Cape Arthur to talk to a builder, decide on a lot and a house plan. I remember that twice we invited another couple to come with us, tho, I can't remember what couple. I always recited the story of Barbara Fritchie as we passed through Fredrick until Erv told me to shut up, he had heard it enough.

We would meet with Mr. Giddings, the man who had developed the community of Cape Arthur, and also lived there. We had the pick of two lots. I was always glad we chose the one we did. We explained to Mr. Giddings the sort of house plan we wanted. Later, as I was looking through an American Home magazine, I found the house plans that was just what we wanted, and I sent it to him. The

plans must have crossed paths for the next day we received the plan he had drawn up. They were identical, except for being reversed and his plan was for a larger building. The cost would be $16000.

The house plan was a rancher, with a large L shaped front room/dining room, a large kitchen with a door opening into the back yard and one to the basement. There was a master bedroom with bath (shower and a tub, for Erv couldn't stand up in a shower), another large bedroom, and a third smaller one. A large bathroom off the hall.

Then there was an enclosed porch at one end of the house, over the garage. We really did enjoy that porch! It was not heated, but some days the sun warmed it. We didn't use it much in the cold winter months.

The lot was 100' x 200' and slightly inclined so that the driveway was dug out and had concrete retaining walls on each side sloping to the road. The basement opened out to the driveway. There were 6 steps, a walk (under the big bay window) and then 6 more steps to the front door. The big bay window looked out to the front yard.

We were so fortunate that Dad was there to be overseeing the building—making sure only the necessary trees were cut and making sure drains pipes were put around the foundation. (My Dad knew all about that sort of thing.)

In February 1960 we moved into our new home at 300 Arundel Beach Rd, Severna Park, MD, 21146. I remember how big it seemed! It echoed. The furniture from a 4room bungalow was lost in this big rancher. I was proud of the hardwood floors, and I didn't want them covered so we had rugs put down. The walls were plaster and not wallboard so picture hanging was not such a problem. We chose painted walls and tiled bathrooms and kitchen. I really was in my gory making curtains and drapes etc.

The thing, I fondly remember, is telling the folks back in Cleveland that I was hanging out clothes in February and they were still having snow.

Cape Arthur was a waterfront community on the Magothy River. There was a wonderful sandy beach; a shallow area for playing, a deeper area for diving and swimming and two piers for docking boats. There were "boat slips" one rented to dock a boat—small or large depending on the size of your boat. We were living in an ideal vacation community!

Dad had a 14' outboard motor boat. Erv thought we should have a larger motor for that size boat so using our little motor and Dad's motor, Erv traded for a 40 hp motor. Now, we could race up and down the river, but best of all we could tour all the little inlets and creeks off the Magothy. I learned to water ski, but had to wear a bathing hat to keep my glasses on. It was great fun!

Cape Arthur also had a large playground with a tennis court and some playground equipment for the children.

Severna Park was a city situated between two rivers, the Severn River to the west and the Magothy River to the east. It was once a big summer vacation spot with cottages lining the shores. Route 2 (Ritchie Hwy) brought vacationers from Baltimore to the north and from Annapolis and areas to the south. It has grown and many communities had developed along the banks of the two rivers. Cape Arthur was one such community on the Magothy River. It boasted "the best beach." The Cape Arthur Beach really was The Best Beach Around!

Folger McKinsey Elementary school was within walking distance for all the children, but best of all, it was right behind our back yard. What better location could there be for a family with two children? Our back yard connected to Folger McKinsey school's playground. How great was that? We didn't worry about street traffic etc. We knew they were safe and we knew where they were. I was jealous when my nextdoor neighbor, Mary Johnson, would whistle for her girls to come home. I couldn't whistle but, not to be out done, I happened to have a cow bell and would ring it for Ricky and Laurie.

There were two little girls living next door and two little boys living two and three houses down. One day Laurie was 2 doors down playing with the bigger kids when she fell off a glider, breaking her arm. What's with this child—that's two arms broken. I guess I failed to tell of the first. She was two. I had just bathed her and had set her on the toilet seat while I dashed around the corner to get something from her room. She slid off the seat and broke her arm (I think it was the right arm) the doctor said it was a "green stick break." She was in a cast, I don't remember how long, but she used that cast to get Ricky to do her bidding.

I wish it were possible to tell about all the things my children did that made me love them so much. We played together a lot— coloring books, reading, building blocks, cars, games and of course there was the beach (they quickly learned to swim).

We joined the Cape Arthur Improvement Association. There were fees that gave us access to the beach and boat slips. There was a deepwater area for the diving board and swimming area with a lifeguard in the summer. The very shallow beach area was great for the toddlers and nonswimmers. It was Langrila, again!!

We attended the association meeting and I joined the Women's Club. The first meeting I attended everyone was very nice and welcomed me. But there was one woman in particular that was especially nice and I wanted to be sure and remember her name. Her name was Beth Slicker. That should be easy—slicker one wears them in the rain. The next time I saw her I could only think of raincoat. So much for association.

Mother and Dad lived less than a mile away, on Marie Avenue. Their nextdoor neighbor was the Jernigan family, Bob and Joanne and sons Robin and Jimmy who were Ricky's age. We would team up with Bob and Joanne when the Association had dances or parties. Mother and Dad often joined us. They were fun and the three men enjoyed concocting pranks to play on each other.

In October, Halloween Trick or Treat was always between 7 and 8, followed by a bonfire and goodies at the playground.

Mother and other Garden Club ladies would decorate the lamp poles and signs at Christmas (with help from the spouses) and Mother helped judge the Christmas Doorways. It was a family community!!

Chapter 8 • 1962, Back to Work

"Strive not to be a success, but rather of value."
—Albert Einstein

The children were getting older and I was feeling the need to get back to work. Ricky was in school, we registered Laurie in Kindergarten, and I went job hunting. Upon asking Dr. Landmesser, the doctor who handled Laurie's broken arm, if he knew where to begin, he suggested I check with a private Physical Therapy office there in Annapolis. I couldn't believe the hospital did not have a Physical Therapy Clinic. (I had always worked in a hospital environment.)

I was interviewed by Bill Rhoads, one of the owners of The Belvedere Rehabilitation Institute. I was hired and was to work on Mondays, Wednesdays and a half day on Fridays. His partner, Jim Barnhardt, didn't approve because I was a woman. Didn't he know this was a woman's profession first, before men joined the business?

Their main office was in Baltimore and they were branching out. The Annapolis office was on Cathedral St. about a block from The Anne Arundel Hospital. The office was in a building that had been a large old home but now housed our PT Department as well as four doctor's offices. We were in the basement. There was an office, a waiting room, bathroom and a long treatment room with a row of 6 plinths (treatment tables) which were separated by curtains. Our equipment consisted of a large whirlpool tub (for legs) a small whirlpool tub (for arms and hands), a diathermy machine, an ultrasound machine, a small and a large infrared lamp, a paraffin bath tub, for hands, and a hot moist packs tub, and a cubicle for cervical traction. I was very familiar with all the equipment, except the Ultrasound machine. I knew infrared penetrated deeper than a light bulb. I knew diathermy was an electrically inducted heat and not used if there was any metal inside the person, (rods to repair fractures etc.) but I didn't know what an ultrasound machine did. It was a new modality for me. The sound waves penetrated more deeply into the tissue and seemed to have an antiinflammatory action on the injured muscles. Diathermy was being used less and less. Fortunately, I didn't need a special class to learn to use the new modality. It became a regular part of almost every treatment—heat, ultrasound, massage and exercise. All adjusted to each patient's diagnosis.

It was Bill who ran the Annapolis office along with me being there part time. Jim was in Baltimore. I greatly admired Bill for his Physical Therapy knowledge and skills. He was charming and smart and could retain information to every detail. He came back from a lecture one day and recited all the statistics verbatim. Amazing!

Again, I can't remember dates, but it wasn't long (maybe, a year) before Jim bowed out of the partnership and Bill took on Ernie Burch and then Wilmer Loomis. That was when it became Burch, Rhoads, & Loomis PA. Ernie manned the Baltimore office and Mr. Rhoades (part time) and Mr. Loonis (back then, we never used first names) were in Annapolis. The business grew and it soon became apparent we needed more room, as did the doctors who shared our old house. They consorted together and bought a building near the hospital. The address was Murray Avenue and that was the parking lot, but the building itself was on Shaw Street an easy walk to the hospital.

We were often called to treat patients in the hospital and it was a long haul carrying the 40lb ultrasound machine 2 blocks. More and more doctors were recognizing the importance of Physical therapy. They realized the body's need to exercise to keep moving and to keep flexible and that heat would ease the pain. So, the hospital generously gave us a closet to house an ultrasound machine, a heat lamp and a moist pack tub.

Now you've heard the business end of my job. I always thought it would be fun to just tell about all the silly and funny things that occurred during my PT years. So, here are some of the fun times I remember.

We had PT aids who would bring in the patient and get him or her set up with the hot packs. At the end of 20 minutes she would remove the packs and get the patient ready for the rest of the treatment. One day Bill was told his lady was ready. It was her back and he would give her a back massage. When he went into the booth, she was lying face down with the towel draped across her hips so he could massage her back. She had butterflies tattooed on both buttocks.

When one of Bill's lady patients told him how much she enjoyed the articles in Playboy Magazine he was very interested. She said she would bring him a couple magazines. He was so pleased and was looking forward to her next treatment. When that day arrived and she gave him the magazines, he went off to look at them. As he quickly turned the pages, he was shocked and disappointed. She had torn out all the center fold pictures.

A nice little old black man came in one day with a painful back. He also came with a very bad odor. The aide suggested that before he returned for his next treatment he should bath. before leaving his house. The next time he arrived he was almost white—he had dusted himself all over with powder.

Rearend collisions and whiplash injuries were becoming a common thing. This involved hot packs, ultrasound, massage and cervical traction. Visualize a very small cubicle with a table, a chair and a turkey scale hanging above it. The patient would sit in the chair with arms (if they chose) on the table, with a halter under the chin and the back of the heat and two straps reaching up to a bar hanging from the scale, we would pull the straps until the scale indicated the amount of poundage that would lift and separate the cervical vertebra thus relieving the pressure on the nerves. Later years the device was much more sophisticated, with a motor that would raise to the designated weight and could be intermittent.

We had a young aide who had been working only a short time. She had brought in a cute young black man and we got him all set up in traction with a bell timer. She was to keep an eye on him and release the traction when the bell rang. When it rang, she went back and found him sitting there hanging, with his eyes rolled up, whites showing. She was so alarmed she stared yelling. We all ran back to see what was wrong and found him laughing. He was fine. He had really pulled a fast one on that poor aide! But you know, I have had nightmares about leaving someone in that traction and forgetting about them.

Much later traction was done lying in a supine position with the traction machine connected to the plinth. There was a traction machine at both ends of the plinth so pelvic as well as cervical traction could be done. I recall only one patient that got both cervical and pelvic traction at the same time.

When medical records became a big issue with Medicare and other insurances, Bill was at his worst, a wonderful therapist but an absolutely terrible record keeper. Government was clamping down, and his reluctance to keep records made it necessary for Ernie and Wil to remove him from the business. That was a sad time.

We seldom saw Mr. Burch, but Mr. Loomis (now Wil) was in charge of the Annapolis office. He was a wonderful boss, caring and fair, but also a prankster and always telling corny jokes. April Fool jokes were his specialty. He would tell the new aide that she had a phone call from a Mrs. Fox, then give her a phone number to call. When the person on the other ed answered it would be the ASPCA. So, one day we turned the tables. Peggy, a past employee and recipient of his pranks, was asked to be on the other end of the line. Mr. Loomis was told a Mrs. Parrot had called. We gave him Peggy's phone number. When he called, she answered with "Polly wants a cracker." So he got his come uppance.

It was Miss Pretense who gave us the most enjoyment and the biggest laugh. Wigs were a fad back then and one of the aides had worn one to work but found it too hot. She placed it over a can in the bathroom. While Mr. Loomis was treating patients over at the hospital Peggy (a prankster too) took the wig, a back brace and made a body on a plinth. It looked just like a body lying on its side, there were even impressions of the heels. We asked Dr Landmesser (also a prankster) to tell Mr. Loomis there was a patient he wanted him to see when he got back at the office. (Dr. Landmesser often designated a therapist to see a patient.) When Mr. Loomis returned to the office, Debbie handed him a clipboard with the patient's name (Miss

Pretense), her diagnosis and what to treat. He rolled his chair into the booth and we heard him say "Miss Pretense" no answer, a pause "Miss Pretense," still no answer. He daren't touch her. Then we (who are standing outside the booth) hear him roll his chair, open the curtain and start to say "Peggy." When he saw us standing there, barely controlling our laughter, he knew the joke was on him. He could take it as well as give it.

Searching for help for Laurie

We were still on Murray Ave when I began my search for something to help Laurie. She was in so much pain! A physical therapist by the name of John Barnes was conducting seminars on a new concept in treating pain—Myofascial Releases & Cranial Sacral Therapy. Since pain is so often connected to tightness and restrictions in the muscles and tendons, and since the Myofascia is the connective tissue holding everything in place, one could relieve the pain by releasing those restrictions. So, I began attending every seminar I could get to. I learned this new concept was a handson sensing of that very tightness. I found I could feel that tightness release and move and I would follow it until all the tightness had relaxed. It was exciting! Many therapists and doctors were very skeptical but I was lucky that my bosses let me use the technique.

I remember one of my first patients was a young high school girl. Her mother came into the booth with her. She was having pain in her right hip and leg. When lying on her left side she could not (abduct) raise the right leg without pain. I did some myofascial releases to the (adductors) inside of her leg and when asked to, again, lift her leg it went flying to the ceiling. Her Mother gasped and we all laughed joyously. You know I was just as surprised as they were. My first big success!

I read a lot and discovered another new technique, Trigger Point Therapy in conjunction with Myofascial Pain. I bought the book Myofascial Pain & Trigger Point Therapy by Janet Travel. To release a trigger point, one needed to agitate the point sight; doctors could inject it with a needle, and then stretch; or a therapist could knuckle it (it hurt) and then stretch. The stretching was most important and her book had diagrams showing how to stretch each muscle.

The most important thing I learned was that the trigger point for the pain was in a muscle but that muscle could be in an area opposite the pain. That the restrictions in tissue opposite the pain were causing the painful area to have to work harder and strain against the tightness. As we discovered in my first patient.

It was such fun, at family gatherings with my nephews, nieces, etc. They would say "my shoulder hurts" and I would press a trigger point, then stretch the arm. Voila, they could move the arm without pain!

The real point to all this was "Could I help Laurie?" She saw a lot of doctors, had all the tests available, but no scientific reason could be found for her pain. Many doctors said it was all in her head. Some called it Fibrositis, that's an inflammatory condition of the muscles, but there was no inflammation. Finally, in 1980 the American College of Rheumatology confirmed that this pain so many of their patients were exhibiting was a real entity and called it Fibromyalgia and established specific criteria for diagnosing it. Happily, the patients were no longer considered hypochondriacs. They had a name for their pain! That was great, but how do they get relief from that pain? There was no known cause and no known remedy. Many different pain killers were on the market; such as Tylenol, Motrin, and some narcotics. There was also Myofascial Releases, Cranial Sacral Therapy and Trigger Point Therapy.

Erv and I decided that Laurie should come home for a week. I would drive to Paole, PA, where she could be treated by John Barnes himself. She would be able to receive several treatments before flying back to Texas. I was not driving at night so my good friend Marge Loomis volunteered to do the late driving. She was such a blessing! I don't remember just how many trips Laurie made back home. Unfortunately, the treatments did not change how Laurie was feeling. She was so brave and strong with it all.

It was nice having her home for these short visits. It was a bonding time for her and her Dad. He felt so sorry and helpless and catered to her every wish. They were good for each other. He was in pain too.

Something good did come from those trips. I was watching as John treated Laurie. He would talk and I would learn, then I would go back and apply it in my work. I was realizing my patients were getting relief from their pain.

One day, John said, if I would write an article for the P T Forum, a newspaper for physical therapists, I could attend one of his seminars free. What an opportunity! All I had to do was tell about my experience using this new method of treating pain. Piece of cake! It was published and I attended another of John's seminars. How about that! Moi? I was a pioneer. I was among the first using this new treatment. And it *was* a NEW treatment concept!!

Chapter 9 • Fun and Adventures with Family

"Keep your face always toward sunshine, and
shadows will fall behind you."
—*Mark Twain*

Every Thanksgiving and Easter we traveled the Pennsylvania Turnpike back to Cleveland to see the Ohio family. When the Ohio Turnpike was completed the trip was easier. There were Plazas along the way where we could pull over for gas or a potty stop or a bite to eat. I remember the time we were traveling on Christmas Eve and we stopped at one of the Plazas. It was all decorated for Christmas with trees, and bells, and greenery, and Christmas music filled the air. We had Christmas dinner with all the fixings—It was so homey and I felt all warm and happy, and we were all together.

We always stayed with Mom and Dad. The relatives and friends would come to visit. The Kendels always came and of course Alma, Lillian and their families. We would sit around the living room and look at each other and talk. Erv would take off and visit his buddies from work—especially Dick Sopko. It still bugs me as I remember about it. I was left alone with the children and nothing to do. I always brought a lot of games, puzzles and cutouts for us to pass the time. Mom and Dad were always great. But it was boring.

It was tough trying to see everyone and please everyone. Alma or Lillian would want us to come to their home for dinner. One year, after church, when we all sat down at Mom's bountiful table she said, "now don't eat too much you have to go to Alma's for dinner." All that good food and don't eat too much? We never let her live that one down!

As the children grew Ricky took the navigator seat. He loved to identify the cars— especially the Station Wagons. Station Wagons were new on the market. You were just beginning to see them and Ricky watched for them. We ladies had the back seat. Once Laurie learned to read there was no need to entertain her—just give her a book.

The Thanksgiving trips could be a bit hairy considering the weather that time of year. One year it was raining and the roads were getting slick, we watched the car in front of us slide sideways off the road. There could be snow too but we always made it home safe and sound. Though, I don't know how sound I was when we got home. Erv was an excellent driver but fast and not always patient. On the trips home we would leave the Pennsylvania Turnpike and get on the 2 lane mountain roads. He would pass a truck or a car and I would be stressed out. I remember getting home, the house would be cold, I would be tired, and I would be very disagreeable. Sorry Guys!

Another trip, after my dad died, my mother went with us. By then the police could track your speed from the other direction and send word to another up the road. Erv was pulled over for speeding. We had to follow the police to a little town off the highway and pay the fine. He was kidded mightily about that.

It was always fun to stop at the Plaza and look around—buy postcards, candy and magnets. They had magnets of every state in the Union. I began collecting them and putting them on my refrigerator. Years later Charlotte gave me a map of the US that stuck to the fringe—It was for the State magnets. I wanted to see our country first so began collecting one for each state. Then, as I visited each state, I would put the magnet on the map. In the end there were only 4 states that had no magnets—Hawaii, North Dakota, New Mexico, Kansas.

My Mother and Dad lived just around the corner, well, 2 blocks up and then around the corner. Not far. It was comforting having them so close. Especially on the days I worked. When I first went back to work Ricky was in 2nd grade and we had enrolled Laurie in Kindergarten We hired a babysitter, Helen, to be there for them after school. Knowing my folks were so close was such a comfort.

I don't remember just how long we had Helen with the children. It was probably when she could no longer come. Instead of finding someone new we decided the children would be ok on their own. School was just in our back yard, they had not far to go. Ricky was responsible and my folks were just around the corner.

When we moved to Maryland Erv had chosen St. Paul's Lutheran church in Annapolis for us to attend. It was of the Missouri Synod as Erv was raised. We attended every Sunday and the children went to Sunday school. They joined the Walther League—the Lutheran youth group. They endured 2 years of catechism and a quiz in front of the congregation before they could be confirmed. Poor kids! But they were both smart and did well.

I remember one Sunday, Erv had gone to pick them up from Walther League. I was sitting watching TV when I saw something scurrying across the drapes over the doorway leading to the porch. The night before I had been awakened by some noise and on investigating, I discovered a little animal sitting on Laurie's dresser. I thought it was her Gerbil but when it moved—it sort of soared down to the floor and ran down the hall to the front room. It was a flying squirrel that had gotten in through the fireplace.

Everyone was awake by now but we shut all the bedroom doors and went back to bed. In the morning we looked all over but found not a trace of it. Now, here it was running across the curtain rods. Well, when the gang got home, we sent Ricky over to my Dad's for a crab net and a box trap. By the time he was back, the little thing was inside the TV works. My smart Hubby had a good plan. We would take the TV out of its cabinet and set it on a sheet. Pull the sheet up all around it and carry it out to the porch it was raining heavily so we couldn't go outside with it. Ricky got down and unscrewed the TV, and carried it out to the porch and set it on the table. We opened the outside porch door, unwrapped the TV and hoped the animal would go outside. Dumb animal—it went in the other direction to the

wrong end of the porch. So, Ricky took a broom and chased it outside. What an adventure!

There was always a big celebration for graduations and confirmations. All the families from Cleveland came and the Kendels and of course the folks here. We had the enclosed porch and a lovely back yard and the school playground—they were happy occasions!

Ricky joined Cub Scouts and I became a Cub Scout Leader. It was fun but I had different ideas than some. No cut and paste stuff for us. We made an SOS transmitter, and with my Mother's aid made a cute little ceramic fish toothpick holder. (I still have it.)

One day I drove them to the head of Severn Run, hoping to see the fish spawning. There were no fish, but the hike along the creek was fun. There were 2 boys that were always disruptive and, even tho, I spoke with their mother I had no control. It was sad, that we know about ADD and other childhood problems. I was ignorant back then and was very annoyed with them. Poor kids. I wonder what they are doing now.

Laurie did Brownies and went into Girl Scouts. I wasn't much involved with that except for a campout she wanted to go on. Erv wouldn't let her go unless I went too. It was embarrassing for both of us. I felt like a fifth wheel. He was such a worry wart when it came to his daughter.

Perhaps it was from watching me sew her dresses that Laurie became interested in sewing. Yes, I made most of her dresses when she was real little and, later, we even had look alike dresses. It was fun wearing them.

She had a friend who liked to sew too. One fall they were busy making Barbie doll clothes and sold them around the neighborhood. I marveled at how they had the dexterity to sew on the tiny snaps and buttons.

Ricky and Laurie both did well in High School. Ricky was listed in the book of outstanding students. He was involved with all the sound and lighting for the dramas, other events. He was almost late for his own graduation because he was setting up the sound system.

Laurie became involved with the Youth For Christ group. It was a wonderful Christion group, meeting after school and at different homes. It was there that she met Greg Skalla.

While all this was going on with the children there were things happening within the larger family

In 1962, County Trust Co, the bank that brought my father to Annapolis and consequently to Cape Arthur and brought us to Maryland, merged with a Baltimore bank, Baltimore National. They became Maryland National Bank. In a way it was a blow to my Dad. He no longer had the intimate, friendly relationship with the branches that he once had. On the other hand, it was a financial bonanza, for the bank stock paid off well. It enabled him and Mother to build their dream house. How grand was that? Mother often remarked, "it is the home we should have had when raising 4 children." This home was spacious enough for children and grandchildren to all get together. And we did, on many occasions.

Dad had a bad heart. When he would overdo physically, he needed a nitroglycerin pill. He never told Mother but would call to tell me. He didn't want Mother to worry but needed to tell someone. He would also call me when he was playing a joke on Mother.

He loved to take photos. Just for fun, he took pictures of the centerfolds of Playboy magazine. One day, when Mother was to show slides of their trip to GA and the azaleas to her Garden Club, she asked him to set up the carousel for her. He mischievously included several extra of his own. Of course, he called to tell me all about his mischief. That evening when I got home from work, I went over to see how Mother had reacted. I walked in, looked at Dad who just shrugged. Mother was not giving him the satisfaction of fussing. I finally said "Mother, what happened?" Then she laughed and said, "One of the women said, I wouldn't have believed this from Delbert." She turned the tables on him and that was as much a joke as the one he pulled.

Erv served in many capacities at the bank. He was a Cashier. He was an Assistant Manager. He was an Auditor and a Vice President. When he was auditing auto dealers, he discovered a dealer who was pulling a scam, not recording the sale of a car. So, the bank closed the dealer down and sold the remaining cars at manufacturer's price. Erv was able to let Maurice know about a deal for a camper. Maurice bought it. He and Miriam had many a trip across country in that little camper.

While Erv was Assistant Manager at the Annapolis office he thought it would be fun to have a Christmas flower show. The gals would bring in their Christmas flower arrangements; there would be judging and a prize. My Mother would be the judge for she was good at that sort of thing. The gals all enjoyed it, especially when their pictures got into the newspapers. It was good publicity, too

There was the time, too, when he was trying to lose weight and was eating a lot of eggs. He had forgotten to take the hardboiled egg with him so called and asked me to bring it to him. I grabbed an egg out of the fridge and did just that. Later that afternoon he called me. "What did I think I was doing?" "What do you mean?" I said. "The egg was raw!" he replied. Seems he held it over the wastebasket to peel it and when he cracked it, it was raw! His desk was in a large room with lots of other desks and gals were watching. They all laughed—was I trying to tell him something? (Raw eggs were believed to be aphrodisiac).

Mother and Dad traveled a lot. We would keep an eye out on their place and I would go over and water her violets.

Ricky helped Gramma with the weeding and was a big help when Grandpa put in a sprinkling system. Dad, in turn, came over and helped Erv, also, put in a sprinkling system. Dad was the brain not the brawn.

One summer when Erv's Dad and Mom and Ray and Alma came from Cleveland, Dad arranged a fishing trip for the guys. Erv's Dad loved to fish. He couldn't have been happier. He and Ray were beaming when they returned with a string of rock fish. We have pictures of the fish laid out on the driveway wall.

It was a Monday in February 1967. Erv was at Rotary. When I got home, from work,

Dad called to invite the kids and I over for buckwheat cakes and sausage. (It was a favorite thing for us to do.) I was to stop and pick up the sausage on our way over. When we arrived there my Dad was dead. He had carried papers out to the curb. When he got back and was sitting at the kitchen table he said "everything is black." That was it. We learned later he had had a massive infarction. I still feel a shock remembering it

Mother had just had bilateral cataract surgery and we were all worried about her, but she was her usual strong self and told us, in no uncertain words, not to fuss over her.

In 1970, Ricky graduated from High School. He chose to attend Virginia Polytechnical School and State University in Blacksburg, VA. Cousin Glenn Davis was attending there and thought highly of the school. It was a good school for engineering and Ricky wanted to be an engineer. With the fun experiences he had had in high school he decided on Electrical engineering.

VPI had a 5year work/study program. The first four years each quarter alternated academic and work. There was no summer break. The 5th year was back on campus doing academics only.

We were so happy to have him home for the work quarters. He had been connected to an engineering consulting group in Baltimore. He was not happy with the first job, but the second job saw him through to the end and gave him a permanent job after graduation.

When Laurie turned 16, she spent the summers working as a Candy Striper at the hospital in Annapolis. Her schedule was the same as mine and I was working just around the corner from the hospital, so we were able to drive together. It was very convenient. She loved the work! So, it was no surprise when she told us she wanted to become a nurse. June 1974 Laurie graduated from high school and headed toward a nursing career.

Through the Youth For Christ meetings, Laura had developed a deep Christian faith that followed her through her whole life. When searching for a college she found a Lutheran college in Hickory, North Carolina, Lenoir Rhyne. It boasted an excellent Nursing School. Perfect! We packed up my old steamer trunk and drove her to Hickory, NC.

The years that followed were filled with many happenings! The children were able to attend most of them.

On June 26, 1972 Erv's folks (Nany and Papa) celebrated their 50th wedding anniversary. We all congregated at Lillian's home for the big celebration. Lots of food, prepared by the daughters Alma and Lillian. But I am sad to report many of us got food poisoning. Erv had taken Nany and Pap home and Rick was driving Laurie, my Mother and me. I was the first to get sick and we had to pull over so I could throw up. We drove a bit farther when Ricky, Mother and I were all sick. Ricky pulled over to the curb so Laurie, who was ok, could walk up to a High's Store and call Erv. He came and drove us to the hospital. When we arrived there, we found Dick Sopko sicker than all of us. What a time! The girls felt so bad about the food. But, interestingly, when Rick, Mother and I were out on the curb throwing up, only a motorcyclist stopped to help. Then a policeman saw us and stopped. He asked where we had eaten. We had to tell him. We stayed at Nany's an extra night before driving home.

It was good we celebrated that year, for Papa had developed cancer and died the following February. We had gone out earlier to see him when he had been in the hospital. He was embarrassed by the nurses caring for him and didn't want Laurie to become a nurse. He didn't want her to be caring for men. Too bad he didn't know she would become a pediatric nurse.

 In September 1972, Aunt Beryl (my dad's sister and our favorite Aunt!) threw a big Family Reunion at Nemacolin at Deep Creek Lake. All her nieces and nephews and their families were present. It was a grand time!

You ask, who was Aunt Beryl? She was a spinster until age 40 and then married an old sweetheart, Gus Gortner. (Rumor has it that Grandma didn't approve of Gus and discouraged their relationship. She finally did marry him.)

As I was growing up, she and my grandfather lived next door. She taught me to knit and when I was 14, she tried to teach me to drive. There was no automatic transmission then and I had to learn to shift gears. After I stripped the gears a couple of times, she gave up.

She enjoyed spoiling her nieces and nephews. There were 4 of us at that time. She was brave enough to take us all to the circus. She doted on us. When she married Uncle Gus, they bought a farm outside of Oakland and raised beef cattle. I was off to college but my younger brother and sister enjoyed spending vacations with them, on the farm.

When Erv and I moved to Maryland we would drive to the farm every spring just to buy maple syrup— that was the excuse. We might visit the neighboring farms to see how they taped the trees and made the syrup. Did you know it takes 25 to 75 gallons of sap (depending on the sugar content) to make one gallon of syrup? It was always an adventure! It would be early spring and the weather unpredictable. One trip we awoke to head home and found the roads were full of snow and no tracks or plows ahead of us. Erv was a very good driver and we got through the snow and off the mountains to clear roads. That is what one would expect in the mountains of Garrett County.

My mother and Erv's Mother both had birthdays in March. So, on the 15 of March 1973, we celebrated my Mother's 75th, then drove to Cleveland to celebrate Erv's Mom's 80th on the 17th. Those milestones need to be remembered and celebrated.

Erv's Dad had been dead only a few months when Easter arrived. We all thought it would do Nany good to get away, take a trip down to see us. It was a good idea! She flew down by herself, and stayed about a week. We took her to see the Cherry Blossoms at the Tidal Basin in

Washington. They were so beautiful! It was fun taking pictures and
 watching Nany enjoy the beautiful trees. We enjoyed having her, too.

Our 25th wedding anniversary arrived that June 26, 1973. The folks from Cleveland, that included the Kendels, came to celebrate. The families had joined together to buy us a silver "tea set" which included a large silver tray, a tea pot, a coffee pot, sugar bowl and creamer. (We needed that like a hole in the head) but we were thrilled to have such lovely silver!!? There was another gift I must tell about. Erv had a cousin Edna, who was a bit of a snob. When we opened her gift, we all starred, gasped and wondered, "What is it?" It was silver alright, but it was about 6 inches long and shaped like a horse's penis. We weren't familiar with parmesan cheese shakers.

One can always find humor in almost any situation.

It was in 1973, I had developed a detached retina, and I was rushed to Johns Hopkins Wilmer Eye Clinic for the surgery. They were doing some upgrading of the facilities and I was in a ward of 5 beds. The bathroom was at one end of the big room and was used by the staff and the occupant of a private room down the hall. After the surgery both of my eyes were bandaged. I couldn't see, but my ears were very tuned to all the sounds. I was lying quietly in bed when I heard footsteps and someone whisper, "Mmmisss Laaaangg." Not feeling up to any conversation I ignored it. Then later, I again hear footsteps and someone whisper, "Mmmisssss Laaangggg." This time I answered, "Yes?" There was no response. Strange! Several more times I heard footsteps and "Mmmissss Laaaanggg" with still not response.

The next day when the bandage on the good eye was removed, I heard footsteps again and popped my eye open. A woman was walking into the room and toward the bathroom. She opened the door, walked in and as the door was closing it whispered "mmmiissss laan-nggg." Here, all along, I was saying "Yes?" to a bathroom door!

The following year I needed cataract surgery on both eyes. At that time, inserts were only for the elderly for the young were too active. Thank goodness for contact lenses!! (Who wanted to wear the big thick magnifying glasses?)

Rick and Laurie were already wearing contacts so knew all about them. One evening as I was removing the lenses, one lens got stuck and I could not get it out. Rick suggested I stick my face in a sink of water—maybe it would float out.

But Laurie remembered her friend, a neighbor, had a suction cup to remove contact lenses. Her friend was happy to oblige and all was well.

Erv & I were quite a pair! He with a wooden leg that had to be taken off at night. Me with contact lenses that had to be taken out at night. One night after he had removed his leg and I had taken out my eyes and we were settled in bed, there was a loud knock on the door. I turned to Erv, "are you going to put your leg on or shall I put my eyes in?" I don't remember who did what but it has been a good story for many years.

Time was passing too fast. The children were growing older, getting on with their lives. In 1974 Rick (It is Rick now) was going into his 5th year at VPI. He would be settled at the university for the next year. He decided it was time to marry his high school sweetheart, Eileen Moran. Erv and I hosted the Rehearsal Dinner at our house. We catered the meal but Erv's roses were the big hit. They were so beautiful and he was so proud of them.

The wedding was outdoors on the lawn of Pasadena United Methodist Church. The bride was beautiful, the weather was perfect. It was all so very lovely. It was small and intimate with mostly just families present. The reception was in the church fellowship hall. I admired the couple for their wisdom when they decided on a small wedding. Eileen's parents had given them a set amount of money to spend as they wished. A small wedding meant money for a honeymoon or a grocery bill. I'm sure Rick had also planned ahead for this time without a job. So, they moved into a little trailer near the campus at Va Tech. Eileen found a job at the school library and they had the "green stamps." They did fine! We were so proud of them. The fact that Rick had put himself through college was even more reason to be proud!

1974 was also the year we drove Laurie to Hickory, NC to begin her nursing career. We packed up my Old Trunk with everything she would need—summer and winter. She was far from home and would leave the trunk there when home between semesters. Good old trunk!

Erv was becoming more involved in Rotary. Their Annual Oyster/ Bull Roast, every February, was a big important fundraising event. Even though he was treasurer for only one year, being the banker, he was always responsible for the money. He also sold the most tickets. (He was a regular at the American Legion Hall near our home and had all those members buying tickets.)

Rotary was important to him. He would never miss a meeting, which was every Monday for dinner. He felt it was good for him and the bank to be with those men.

I joined the Inner Wheel, the wives of the Rotarians. We met just once a month, and for dinner also. The women were friendly enough but I wasn't close to any of them. We weren't on the same social plane and I wasn't a drinker. I needed to be a member, so I could know the people when Rotary had special dinners and the wives were invited.

Erv went through the "chairs" and the year he became president his club had to host some members from Rotary International. He was very nervous and knew he would have to sit at the head table and next to the dignitaries. "What should I talk about?" he asked, as we were driving to the restaurant. Gosh, I'm not good at making small talk, either, so had little to offer, but said, "ask, how was the traffic on Ritchie Hwy?" Really! Was that the best I could offer? What bumpkins we were. But you know, later we often joked about "how was the traffic on Ritchie Hwy?"

Laurie was doing well at Lenoir Rhyne University, making the Dean's list. She made friends too. A little Chinese girl, Shannon, whose Father and Mother were Lutheran Missionaries, living in San Francisco. (They had been forced to leave China). That Easter of 1975 she brought Sharon home for the holidays. Sharon had a sister, Esther, living in NY State (somewhere). It was an opportunity for the two to be together, so we invited her to come stay, too. It

was funny! I wanted to show them the sights of Washington, the capital of their new country. But no—their only interest in Washington was to meet up with a cousin who had married an American Chinese man.

Did you know that Chinese American men went back to China to find a wife? Their cousin was such a wife. It seems the American Chinese women are too independent.

We had fun, tho. We found the cousin's apartment and had a nice visit with her. She showed us pictures of her wedding—a lot of red. Interesting. We didn't meet the hubby, but there was a baby boy, named Goulda. They wanted to go into China Town and buy some special Chinese food, but I wasn't sure that was such a good idea since I didn't know my way around that area. So, we came home. They were very happy to be able to see their cousin again. I can imagine how it must feel, when one is far from home, to meet up with someone from home.

June 7, 1975! Five Years of work and study! Rick received his BS Degree in Electrical Engineering! We were so proud and happy! We were even happier when he was asked to return to the same job he had as an intern—Gipe Associates Consulting Engineers, in Baltimore. He and Eileen found an apartment and moved to Baltimore. They were near home again. Wonderful!

Erv and I were living the life of empty nesters. We went to work in the morning and returned home in the evening. When he was working in Annapolis, we would often drive into work together. Especially, in the winter, when the roads were bad with snow. We would drive in early and stop at The Maryland Inn for breakfast. We would sit by the fireplace and watch them light the logs with paper and candles from the tables the night before. It was real cozy!

When strawberries were in season, I would stop, on my way home, at the strawberry patch and pick a quart or two. Erv loved strawberries! He would stand at the sink capping and eating, capping  and eating, and saying, "I'm going to break out." He never did.

We really enjoyed our home. There was a tree just outside our kitchen window. We had a little platform on it that was a perfect place where a squirrel could stretch out or look in the window, waiting for Erv to come and put out peanuts. Which he did. He had a little butter tub that he filled with peanuts. He would tap his fingers on the window, then crack open the screen door and place the tub just outside. The squirrel would come down and eat. One day the scamp came inside. So, we placed peanuts on a path, through the house to the back door. The animal followed the peanuts and was soon outside again.

One lovely, warm, afternoon we were standing outside just enjoying life. I looked across the yard and saw this little squirrel coming toward me. He was cute—the way he was hoping and coming toward me. The next thing I knew he had climbed up my dress and was sitting on my shoulder. I hunched my shoulders and turned to Erv, saying "Honey, Honey, Honey." It must have been someone's pet.

Dick and Vi Sopko were becoming regular visitors. They would come in February and again in the fall. February was the Rotary Bull

Roast. Dick, being a CFO, was the perfect helper for money collecting and final tabulations. Vi and I would attend, eat, and enjoy the music. When we all got back home, we would listen to the guys laugh and tell us about the fun they had had.

When they came in the fall, we would take a trip to Ocean City. It was not so crowded then. We always had ocean front rooms where we would sit on the balcony, watch and listen to the ocean. What is it about the ocean that calms the soul? We would drive around and take in the sights and, of course, shop the stores along the boardwalk. It was a must that we stop at Wockenfuss Candy store. I always bought their amazing caramel covered marshmallows. Vi was diabetic and Wockenfuss had the best sugar free candy. Their visits were always fun. When Erv and Dick got together something funny always happened. We laughed a lot!

1976 was Our Country's 200th Anniversary. It was a year of nationwide celebrations. The Tall Ships from many other countries sailed up the Chesapeake Bay on July 4th. What a Sight! We drove to Sandy Point State Park to watch them sail under the Bay Bridge. Then we raced up to Baltimore to watch them come into the Baltimore Harbor. When we knew they were leaving, Mother and I drove up to the Harbor to watch their departure. We stood on Federal Hill watching their departure. The German Ship sailed out with sails furled.

We were so close we waved to the young men standing in the rigging (they looked so young and handsome in their sailor uniforms).

It was so exciting! The other ships were chicken. No sails for them⊠ they motored out of the harbor.

The winter of 1976 was the winter of the BIG FREEZE. Everything froze—We chopped ice at our Cape Arthur Beach so we could feed the duck. Our friends, the

Jernigen's, had moved over to Linsted on the Severn River, and we would go there to ice skate. Their boys would skate across the river to Harold Harbor. Scary! We skated on Lake Waterford, too. There were tales of cars driving out onto the rivers and, of course, some folks tried their hand at ice fishing.

It was during those first 2 years at Lenoir Rhyne that Laurie developed the pain in her hips and legs. The pain was such that she could not sit to study or sit for lectures. She was having a difficult time! She saw doctors but none could find a reason for the pain. Her Physical Therapist Mother wasn't able to help either. I was angry. The best I could do was have a bed tray made that would prop up so she could read and write lying down. She endured and continued her schooling.

Laurie had a boyfriend in high school, Greg Skalla. Their relationship had cooled a bit but I guess absence does make the heart grow fonder for he was the reason she transferred to the University of Virginia. He had only one more year to graduate, when he asked her to marry him. They had it all worked out. He would still be at UVA getting his Masters and she would be finishing her nursing degree. And so, it was, they got married! February 7, 1978.

It was all very exciting; we were the family of the Bride and were responsible for the wedding plans. Erv saw to it that all his little girl's wishes were met. I must say here, that Laurie knew what she wanted. I wasn't much help except to make her veil and my own dress, but I was there to listen, to offer suggestions, give her support. It was a big wedding with a band, sit down dinner, and all. All the folks came from Cleveland. Mom flew down with Dick & Vi. The others drove— Alma and Ray, Lillian and Dave, Norman Gerlat, and Freddie and Helen Kendel, of course.

Now, the wedding was February 7, 1978 when weather was most unpredictable. The guests all arrived; the Sopkos flew down with Nany while the Cousins and Aunts and Uncles drove. The wedding went off according to plans. The bride was beautiful, the Groom was all smiles. They left amid showers of rice, and then it snowed!

The next morning when the Cleveland folks headed home the roads were treacherous. To this day they still talk about Laurie's wedding and their trip home. The best story, tho, was from the Sopko's and Nany. Cleveland was snowed in, their plane was rerouted to Chicago where they spent the night in a hotel. Mom had packed a roast beef sandwich and Dick had taken a duffel bag full of steamed crabs. They carried their treasures with them into the hotel. Mom finally decided the sandwich should not be eaten and threw it in the waste basket, but Dick made sure the crabs got to Cleveland. Vi reported later that she had to do some strong convincing for Dick

to finally agree that, after all that time, the crabs were not safe to eat Bummers! They said Nany was a real trooper through it all. She would be!

June 26, 1978 Erv and I celebrated 30 years of married bliss!!

Alma and Ray, Ray Jr and Glenn came east for a visit. There is so much history here and so many things of interest to see. We tried to show it all to them. The best fun was introducing them to the steamed crabs. They soon got the hang of it and wanted more. The boys cleaned up their empty shells and took them home for Show and Tell.

In early 1978 Rick and Eileen moved to Cape Canaveral, FL. He

had a new job with Statler Stag Associates, anotherelectrical contracting company. Rick especially enjoyed working on the contracts for The Kennedy Space Center. Awesome! They were near Disney World, too.

It was Christmas in sunny Florida for us that year. Rick and Eileen were great tour guides. We toured the Space Center— saw alligators in a pond on the grounds. Eileen took us to Disney World. Orlando is only a short distance from the Cape and on a very straight highway called the Beeline. Along the road we saw armadillos, a strange looking animal. At the Cape Canaveral Port, we saw the pelicans. I was fascinated by the Pelicans; whose bill holds more than its belly can.

There are certain birthdays that should always be specially celebrated. Nany turned 85 on March 17, 1979. It was March, and we weren't sure about the weather, but we made it there! It was a happy celebration at Lillian's house. By then Nany was living on Knickerbocker. She had moved there after Papa died, to be closer to Lillian, who drove her shopping and to all her appointments. (Alma never learned to drive and of course Erv lived too far away.)

When we visited Mom we often ate at Lillian's. Lillian loved to cook, and she was a good cook. Her diners were always special—best china and silver, flower centerpiece she had arranged herself— really elegant! We loved to eat at her house!

Rick and Eileen were expecting in November. The months passed and on November 30, 1979 Daryl Richard Lang arrived.

What a lovely way to begin the new year (1980). We all flew to Florida in March for Daryl's Baptism. Laurie and Greg (the Godparents), my Mother, Erv and I. As I recall all these events, I feel the happiness again. I'm a maudlin old woman.

1980: A dual life

I have found that life will always offer something for which to be happy, but it can also fill your life with sorrow. That summer Mother fell and broke her hip. And Laurie and Greg moved to San Antonio, TX, where her leg and hip pain raised its ugly head again.

Mother was standing outside watching a neighbor cut off a limb from one of her trees. As the limb fell, she turned to step back and fell—We don't know if the twist caused the break and she fell or if the fall caused the break. Whatever.

Mother was hospitalized. We called in Dr. Landmesser, the orthopedic doctor whom I knew well from my work. He felt that if Mother was not in pain, she would do well without having any surgery. I had just treated a lady who had undergone the same treatment and was walking with a cane. Then too, there was some danger with surgery that the anesthesia would cause some brain damage in an older person. I later wondered if we made the right decision. Mother did well with a walker but never used a cane.

She stayed with Erv and Me until she was comfortable with the

walker, then moved back into her own house. The first week or so Aunt Mary and Uncle Edgar, Mother's brother and his wife, came to visit and were with her.

Laurie had graduated and was working at the UVA Hospital. She was a pediatric nurse and loving it. Greg had one more year to get his master's degree. Greg's Mother, Lila, and I decided we would visit them, before they up and move away.

Greg's parents had just divorced and his mother, Lila, had decided to become my friend. Which was fine with me. So, before the children finished school and moved away, we decided to pay them a visit. (I guess it was the spring of 1981.) They were ensconced in a nice little apartment with Tali, their Siamese cat, who was a terror until he was allowed to run loose outside. Laurie had a new jacket with a fur collar. Taly really made a mess of that fur—bad cat!!

It was just a short visit but we toured the historic campus. I'm trying to remember the "Mall." The rotunda at one end was some sort of monument but down the mall was a onestory building serving as dorm quarters for special students. I'm trying to remember the reason it was considered an honor to live there.

Virginia is really a lovely state, peaceful countryside, rolling hills and a section of the Sky Line Drive that traverses the Blue Ridge Mountains. We chose to come home via the Sky Line Drive. We stopped at several overlooks and took pictures, of course.

Upon his graduation Greg was offered a job in San Antonio, TX. Soooo far away. So, they moved to Texas. Laurie soon found a job as a pediatric nurse at a San Antonio hospital. A nurse can often see a difficult situation and speak to a doctor about it. But, it seems, the Hispanic doctors were not open to any suggestions from a nurse. It was very stressful for Laurie.

The pains in her hips and legs raised their ugly heads again... so much so, she had to quit work. It was the old problem—pain on sitting and standing. She saw many doctors; had Xrays, CAT scans; MRIs; blood work. She did it all. No one had an answer. "It was probably all in her head." They would prescribe pain medication, muscle relaxants etc. Perhaps the pills would take the edge off. She spent her days lying on her back or her stomach.

Someone suggested she sign up for "Talking Books" through the Library of Congress. She received a catalog of book titles, authors and synopsis. From this she could order 2 books. They sent her a record player and a record of the narrated book she chose. The package had a 2way address sticker so when she had finished listening to a book, she would send it back and receive another. No cost. How great that was! She also began taking a correspondence course and wanted to write children's books. I'm not sure she really wrote any books, but I do have a little story she wrote. She printed it and put it in a small cover which she made. I do have copies of several articles she wrote, about Talking Books, that were published.

In late 1980, The American College of Rheumatology announced that this painful condition was really Fibromyalgia Syndrome and could be recognized by specific criteria. Now the doctors had a name for it but still didn't know what to do about it.

MY big question was, why can't I help my daughter—I am a trained Physical Therapist who should know about bones and muscles and stuff? I began looking for new techniques for treating chronic pain. I discovered a book, Myofascial Pain and Trigger Point Therapy, by Janet Travell. I discovered a new technique called Myofascial Releases and Cranial Sacral Therapy, by John Barnes. I bought the book and began going to John Barnes seminars. It was a whole new treatment concept! This was a turning point in my life!

This is when I took on a dual life—my home and family, and my work. It was like a big pot of stew—everything all mixed together (even the kitchen sink, haha). So from now on my Memoirs will be a big pot of mixed events.

It was quite an adventure, going to Cape Canaveral for my first grandchild's baptism! As I told you earlier, we were all there, Rick and Eileen and Daryl, of course, Erv, Moi, my Mother, and Laurie and Greg, who were the godparents. (The whole family, which made it even nicer.) Daryl was the cutest little boy and a perfect little Angel through it all. (No, of course I'm not prejudiced).

We enjoyed seeing Rick's new home which was just a few blocks from the ocean. There is something about the ocean, the small waves lapping at the shore or the rolling waves rushing onto the shore, the expanse of it all, as you look at to the horizon and see a speck, maybe a ship, or see nothing but water and blue skies. We took a walk along the beach, looking for unusual shells, but finding only the usual.

The Cape Canaveral harbor was enticing, for there we could watch the pelicans. I really do like to watch them—the bird whose bill hold more that its belly can. The shrimp boats come in there and the pelicans hope for a handout. I kept snapping pictures. They were so much fun to watch.

It was January of 1981 that Mother moved to her apartment in East Port, MD (sort of a suburb of Annapolis, but don't tell Annapolis that). She was doing well living alone and walking with a walker, but the house and property were just too much for her to care for. Two friends from Garden Club were living there and liked it a lot. Bea, her friend, was on the lookout for a 3 bedroom apartment and when one became available, Mother moved in.

The days that followed were exciting, confusing, tiring, full of questions and decisions. Mother was having trouble getting around and she found the prospect of moving overwhelming. She did insist on a 3bedroom apartment; she made the decisions as to what goes and what to give to the children, what to put in a yard sale, what to give to Good Will, and what to trash.

Evenings, after work, I would go help her sort and pack. One evening we were sitting in her Den, sorting things from shelves of little stuff. She was holding a box of ribbons and as she was taking each ribbon out, she slowly pulled it though her fingers before dropping it into a bag. I looked at her and felt so sorry, for this move was not easy.

Mother had four children. Maurice, the oldest, lived in Salisbury, Md—too far to be of much help other than giving advice. Moi, the second in line, lived just around the corner and had most of the responsibility. Charlotte, 10 years younger, lived 15 minutes away, but was very busy with husband and family. Norman is the youngest 14 years younger than I. He lived in Connecticut. It is obvious who is in the best position to take the wheel. Moi, of course. The four of us would collaborate before big decisions were made and all were very compatible about it.

So, one Saturday we had a Yard Sale out of the lower level of Mother's house. Mother was very astute and did the pricing of the items. I was sure glad of that!! We were all there on the actual sale day. Praise the Lord, all went well!!

I don't remember the actual date, but the move went smoothly and we got Mother settled into her new abode. It was in the Watergate

Apartment complex on the West River. There was a balcony that faced the river where she could sit and watch the boats sail or motor up and down. A special night, during the Christmas season, a parade of boats with Christmas decoration and lights would sail up the river. She had a frontrow seat!

Mother was on the first floor and was able to walk down the hall to the entrance. I showed her how to fold the walker and, using it as a cane, and holding onto the railing, go down the steps to the outside. She then was able to walk around the facility—which was nicely landscaped with trees, and a walk by the river with places to sit.

Mother had had a cleaning lady once a week at her old house, Laura Fix. Laura, not only cleaned, she was a real friend, who Mother really looked forward to seeing once a week. Well she continued to help Mother after her move. Mother would tell me that a light bulb needed changing of something was broken, but not to worry, Laura would fix it!

Mother's apartment was not far from where I worked and I wasn't working every day. So, I would take her shopping and to doctor appointments. One day as we were walking down the hall to go to an appointment, Mother was soooo slow! I was impatient for we had to be on time. I kept urging her on—pick up the walker and walk with it. She ignored me. When we got to the car, I noticed she seemed tired. I asked, "are you alright?" She answered, "I didn't sleep too well last night." I really felt guilty for pressuring her so said, "I'm sorry I fused at you." She replied, "That's alright, I just shut my ears." That's MY Mother! She lived there for 10 years.

Have you ever been to Blackwater Fall, WV? The spring of '81, Erv and I drove to Garrett Co. to see Auntie and bring home maple syrup as we did every year. This year, we took Auntie on a trip to Blackwater Falls. It was just a short, day trip.

We had never seen the falls but I had heard a lot about them. Auntie was very happy to show us the way. There was a lodge on the mountain from where you could walk to an overlook to see the river and some of the falls. It was fun traveling with Auntie as she pointed out familiar places along the way. But walking to the falls was too difficult for both Auntie and Erv, so we were content to see what we could from the overlook.

We bought our gallons of syrup (Erv always had to get some for friends) and headed home. We rode home feeling good about spending that time with Auntie, doing something special she enjoyed, too.

We closed 1981 by spending Christmas in Florida with Rick and family. It turned out to be a very memorable Christmas. It was cold, there was a wind, and the electric went out. Eileen wondered how she was going to cook Christmas dinner.

The stove was gas so she could cook on the top burners, but the oven was lit by an electric spark. She wanted to try lighting it with a match, but we unanimously discouraged that. What to do? How about Chinese? And that's what it was.

We bundled little Daryl up and drove to a Chinese restaurant. It really didn't matter what we ate—we had a good time. Daryl in his stroller, next to Eileen's chair, was the star of the moment, as folks stopped to say how cute and well behaved he was. We agreed!

The spring of 1982, we were flooded with photos of the new house the Skallas were building. We could visualize it as it was going up. Laurie would be so excited when she called us on the phone, describing every detail of the progress and of how Greg was doing the landscaping himself. There were pictures of it going up, there were pictures of the interior, there were pictures of Greg, laboring hard, digging or planting. The house was a onestory rancher with attached garage. It had a master bedroom with bath and 2 other bedrooms, a kitchen and front room, and later a family room was added. The final pictures of her home revealed a lovely house shaded by live oak trees. I was looking forward to a visit there.

Auntie was having real problems with her digestive system. Thinking the doctors here were more in tune with the times, Erv and I drove up and brought her down here for testing with a gastroenterologist. The testing was done but I don't remember the outcome of it. I do remember the fun we had while she was here.

Charlotte and I took Auntie and Mother to the National Aquarium at Baltimore Harbor. It was so much fun! We had Mother and Auntie in wheelchairs, with Charlotte pushing Mother and Moi pushing Auntie.

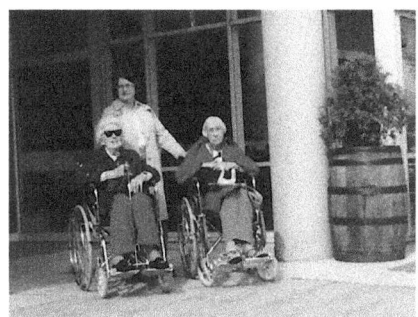

Have you been to the National Aquarium? There are ramps climbing floor to floor and all along the walls are fish tanks with a plaque beside each, telling all about the fish. We were suitably paired for Mother and Charlotte like fish and had to read all the information, while Auntie and I don't really like fish. We didn't bother doing all the reading but we did enjoy watching them. I liked the little seahorses. Auntie and I commented at each tank, at the colors, shapes, the ugly, the pretty, big and little. Always wondering at God's creation of the creatures on this earth. It was a great day!!

The excursion to the Aquarium was not the only fun we had with Auntie. There was her Birthday celebration on April 15. It was a big celebration! It was held at the Wheatley residence. There was C & C and Charlie and Cheryl; M & M with Glenn and Marilyn and her 2 girls and E & E, and Mother. Auntie was so pleased and happy to have all her family around her. Living so far away, this doesn't often happen.

We didn't know, then, that her next visit would be under very different circumstances.

That was in April 1982 and the following September Maurice and Miriam received a call from the Shrocks, the Amish family down the hill from Auntie, saying they are very worried about Auntie, that she needs her family. They had been answering her calls and seeing to her needs, but did not want that responsibility anymore.

Maurice, Miriam and I drove up to get Auntie and bring her back to my house. She could live with Erv and me. She liked Erv a lot, and he thought she was special.

When we arrived, we realized she was in bad shape but before we could really do anything, she had a heart attack and was immediately hospitalized. Now what?

Maurice had to get back to work, so he left and Miriam and I stayed to be with Auntie until she was able to be moved to the hospital in Annapolis.

We had Auntie's car. It was a nice big Pontiac Catalina. (Erv really liked it and Auntie had told him he could have it.) I have to admit, the situation was not good, tho Miriam and I did enjoy the next few days there. We visited the Shrocks and discovered the men were bear hunters. They had a little building where they hung all their trophies. Martha, the wife was a cute little plump lady. She had a mini trampoline on which she exercised. The picture of her little plump body jumping up and down on that trampoline made us laugh. Their 2 daughters were the ones who helped Auntie so much. She would call when she was frightened and they would come up and reassure her. They would help her, too

We also visited several other friends of Aunties whom we also knew. They were all so sorry about Auntie's condition, about her leaving. She was very well known there.

Arrangements were made for her trip to Annapolis, by ambulance. Maurice returned for Miriam and me and we all came home. I'm a bit vague about how it all evolved. Auntie recovered and came to live with Erv and me. We had two extra bedrooms so asked Mother to come and be there, too. Erv and I were both working and gone during the day.

Then one morning I came out of my bedroom to find Auntie on the floor, in the hallway. She was on the way to the bathroom, fell and broke her hip. That was really bad! Off to the hospital she went. She was in a lot of pain but surgery could not be done because of her heart. From the hospital she went to the nursing home. We couldn't take care of her at home. It was so sad! As I look back on that time, I feel so sad and guilty that things couldn't have been different. I realize now, she must have felt so alone, probably frightened, needing comforting. Instead, I was annoyed at her for being grouchy and unappreciative. I would take her special foods but she turned up her nose. She complained a lot, too.

Now that I am old, I realize I should have taken her in my arms and soothed her.

She so desperately wanted to go home to Oakland where all her friends were. We were in the process of getting her back there to a nursing facility when she became very ill and was hospitalized again. I remember Charlotte and I were sitting in the lounge outside of her room when we heard the "code blue" alarm. She died September 7, 1982.

Auntie had her estate in a trust; executed by the bank in Oakland. Her nieces and nephews as well as those on the Gortner side were mentioned in the will. She had designated certain articles to go to specific people and the other things were auctioned off. The trust sent out to each person a list of the articles and they were to return a bid. The highest bidder received the item.

Auntie had already designated that I get a small cherry wood table, an antique lamp and her cedar chest. I bid on other things and received several afghans she had made and 3 of grandma's quilts. Erv got the Pontiac. I continue to have wonderful memories and terrible guilt feelings. I hope she has forgiven me.

Chapter 10 • There is sadness in life

*"When everything seems to be going against you remember
the airplane takes off against the wind, not with it."*
—Henry Ford

As I peruse my photo album, I smile as I recall each event.

Picture this—it is February. It had snowed heavily during the night. Erv had shoveled a path to the road, and was standing in snow above his knees. He had wisely parked one car out at the entrance of the driveway. We were always able to get out once the streets were plowed. Sometimes with snow tires or chains we were out before the plows. Erv loved those adventures.

Life's adventures are like a river. A river begins at its "head waters". Like the Mississippi River, who's headwaters are in northern Minnesota. An adventure flows through life picking up new experiences along the way.

The year 1980 was just that—the headwaters of a big adventure. I think of that year as being the year of significant beginnings. It was the year Mother broke her hip. It was the year Laurie and Greg moved to San Antonia, Tx and the return of Laurie's PAIN. It was the beginning of my search for answers to a treatment for Fibromyalgia and chronic pain.

But...It was, also, a year that the whole family came home for Christmas! Don't you know how it is? When the whole family is together?!!! Such happiness!!

1981

Mother was a trouper. She lived alone in her dream house for a year before moving to Watergate Apartments in East Port, MD.

Laurie and Greg built their new house Erv and I took Auntie to Blackwater Falls.

Greg's mother, Lila, and I had become friends, and one afternoon we drove to the Baltimore Harbor to tour The Constellation. It was moored there and one could tour it. Amazing how sailors endured such close quarters and hardships. That's just the way it was, back in those days.

1981 was also the year we spent Christmas in Florida and had Chinese for Christmas dinner.

1982

Old Man Winter ushered in 1982 with a heavy blanket of snow. The new snows are always so beautiful! The scenes of our back yard and of the front, looking down Arundel Beach road, were post card perfect.

1982 was the year Charlotte and I wheeled Aunty and Mother to the National Aquarium and we also celebrated Aunty's birthday.

A NEW GRANDSON, GERRITT EDWIN LANG! That was the good news from Florida on February 25, 1982. Wow, we now had two grandchildren to spoil.

We anxiously awaited the Christmas holidays when the whole family would be together again and we would meet this new addition to the family.

Every Christmas Erv gave me a large pot holding two poinsettias, a red on and a white one Erv and the children had given me a dishwasher for my birthday and now decided it should be moved near the sink. I was thrilled by what happened next. Erv had a friend from The American Legion who was a builder. He did the remodeling for us. The dishwasher went under the counter next to the sink. The builtin wall oven was removed and all new cupboards, including a corner cupboard with carousel, were installed. There was a microwave, too! Wasn't I just the luckiest gal?

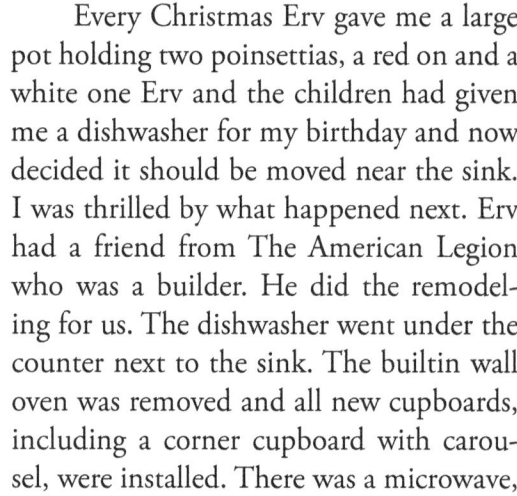

It is interesting, as I page through my albums, I am realizing just how cold our winter used to be. Each year begins with a heavy snow storm; pictures of my back yard with shadows on the snow; pictures of the front driveway with 3 feet of snow to be shoveled; pictures of the monster with ten inches of snow on it. It was all so beau-

tiful, and we were young and could shovel, so enjoyed it. Now, I'm old, and enjoy the warmer winters.

1983

My first trip to see Laurie's new home was in February 1983. The pain in her legs was such that she could only get some relief by lying down. I wanted to see this new house, but I thought too, that maybe I could help her in some way. I guess, just having Momma there was some comfort, but that was the best I could do. We were just beginning to learn about fibromyalgia and myofascial releases and cranial sacral therapy.

I did meet Tali, their cat, and some of their neighbors who were very friendly. I gave their home an A+. They were happy and I could report that back home to Erv.

Mother turned 85 that year. Of course, the family always got together

to celebrate her birthday. She was after all, our family's Matriarch and deserved a celebration. We went to Spiro's Restaurant in East Port. I remember that someone ordered snails uggg!

Christmas was in Florida, but with Roast Turkey, not Chinese

Remember, many chapters back, I told you my life was a mishmash of Family life and Work life? Now, I'm finding it hard to not mix them up. So, bear with me, will you, if I repeat some of the stories?

1984

We were young and ninety seemed like such a very old age, so, it was with amazement and excitement that, in March, we made the trip to Bay Village to celebrate Nany's 90th birthday. We stayed with her in her "little house" where the old clock ticked away and kept Erv awake. He would always stop it when we arrived and start it again as we left.

PROMOTION 1984

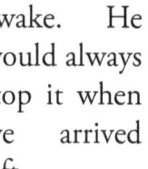

Is it wrong to brag about one's son? That year, Rick was promoted to Chief Electrical Engineer! He had a mustache then! Quite handsome!

I'm looking at some pictures of our yard—the front and the back. I loved our yard, especially in the spring. There were lots of big oaks and several big hickory trees. We had planted several pink Dogwood, and in the back several native white Dogwood would bloom. We had planted azaleas—all colors—in the back, in the front and along the porch side.

At one corner of the patio was the "Monster"—a fireplace built by one of Erv's friends from the American Legion—he was a brick layer. It was hot work and he would quench his thirst with a beer or two. The empty cans would go into the hollows of the brick structure. Well hidden! There was a picnic table, too, with benches. My pride and joy was the planter along the edge that held my 'antique' begonias. They came with me when we moved from Cleveland. They had tiny pink double blossoms like carnations. I would set them out after May 14 and bring them in early in October. The main plant I would repot, after taking cutting off it. The cutting would go into a glass of water, where they would form roots for planting next spring. They would adorn a window sill during the winter.

Remember my telling about the trips Marge Loomis and I made, taking Laurie to Pennsylvania? Our friendships blossomed into full bloom. It reminded me of the friendship Erv and Dick had—when ever we were together, one or the other would do something silly or stupid and we would crack up laughing. We would bike on the B&A Trail; swim at the "Y" here in Severna Park or at the high school on Riva Rd. Sandy always went with us when we went swimming.

Sandy was Marge's daughter and was born with Down's Syndrome. She had a bad hip joint that limited her activities, but she could swim and she was a good swimmer. She had a wonderful sense of humor and it was fun being with her.

Marge's mother lived alone in Philadelphia. There were times when Marge needed to see her and not wanting to make the trip alone, she would ask me to go along. I was helping her as she had

helped me. We were there for each other, though I think she was there for me more than I was there for her.

One sunny day the three of us drove to the Baltimore Inner Harbor to see the boats and enjoy the waterfront. There was a Shopping Mall there, also, that was always enticing, with food courts and restaurants.

That Christmas, 1984, the whole family was together, including my Mother. I remember Daryl saying, "can we go to the playground? It draws me like a magnet!" (What a big people's expression for such a little boy.) The weather was warm and sunny. We climbed and did skin the cat. We slid down the sliding board and teeter totted. I wasn't much good at hand over hand on the bars.

It was a blessing that we were all together, for it was Erv's last.

For some time, I had been concerned about Erv. I'm finding it difficult to explain the change in him. Perhaps it started when the bank installed a computer at everyone's desk. The staff was sent off to a special class on how to use the computer. It was fortunate for those who had a background in typing. It was unfortunate for Erv who could only hunt and peck. He found himself in a position that was beyond his abilities. He was embarrassed.

He was also having trouble hearing and had ordered hearing aids through the VA but hadn't gotten them yet. There, too, was the problem with painful calluses and ingrown hairs on his stump. He was having more trouble walking. He became withdrawn and more quiet than usual. I was worried and at night I would curl up next to him and pray that God would help him and comfort him.

I guess the bank realized the situation, for they asked him to take an early retirement. He would be 60 on his next birthday, April. 26th. So it was. The bank gave him a going away party at the American Legion Hall. Erv was so happily surprised and deeply moved to see his Son, Rick, walk through the door.

In the meantime, the gals in personnel suggested he not take retirement but go for Physical Disability, which would save his bank life insurance. It was a good idea and they set the ball rolling.

Dick and Vi came, as usual, in February for the annual Rotary Oyster and Bull Roast at The Earleigh Heights Fire Station. Erv and Dick were the money men and collected tickets etc. They later, laughing, recounted how "The Judge", who was trying to help, really got in the way. They always seemed to find something to laugh and joke about.

He was in good spirits on the Fourth of July when he invited Marge, Wil, Sandy and Marge's niece to come share steamed crabs with us. Our porch was the perfect place for such a party. Afterward Marge drove us (except Erv) to Baltimore Harbor to watch the Fourth of July fireworks. It was a grand finale to a lovely day!

It was the end of July. Exact dates don't matter. I had attended another of John Barnes's seminars, in Atlantic City, and arrived home Sunday, to find a note from Erv.

He was in the hospital. I was in a panic! Not really reading the note thoroughly I rushed to the hospital in Annapolis. He was not there. It was another frantic trip to North Arundel Hospital where I found him—sooo sick.

He had been to the American Legion and eaten crabs. He had gotten so sick he drove himself to Earleigh Heights Fire Station and asked them to take him to the hospital. (He hadn't wanted the fire trucks with sirens blasting coming to the house.) That is where I found him. I could see he was very sick. They were doing tests, but no answers.

For the first week I went to work, but would hurry back to the hospital afterward and stayed until visiting hours were over. He was too sick to talk. It was a few days later that someone reread the xrays and discovered he had a ruptured diverticulum. He was rushed into surgery. Afterward the surgeon reported that the surgery had been successful. BUT the anesthesiologist looked at me and shook his head—there was a lot of liver damage. I knew then, he would not make it.

I remember standing by his bed, holding his hand. I don't know if he knew I was there or what I was saying but I was trying to send some of my energy into him. The nurses felt sorry for me and brought me a stool to sit on. His kidneys stopped functioning and they wanted to send him to University Hospital for kidney dialysis, but needed my permission. Somehow, I couldn't give it to them. They were doing all sorts of things to help. I watched him swell up like a Macy's Thanksgiving Parade balloon.

My friend Marge was there sitting with me—just having her there was comforting. Then Rick and Laurie were called. They came. The next day I received the notice that his application for Physical Disability had been accepted. That was good news, I would receive his insurance! When I told him, I guess he heard me for I saw him sigh and the next day he died.

The Cleveland folk were notified. They all came; Dick & Vi, Alma & Ray, Lillian & Dave. It's funny, I can't remember if Erv's Mother came.

When I went to The Barranco Funeral Home to take care of the funeral things Erv was not there. When I asked where he was they said the hospital was waiting for my permission to do an autopsy. I should have let them do it but I was irrational and didn't want him cut up any more. Dumb!! Had the diverticula ruptured causing peritonitis?

The funeral was at the Barranco Funeral Home. It was a closed casket. Pastor Eichner from my church gave a fine eulogy. There was another short service at the new VA Cemetery in Crownsville. Erv and I had talked about it and he had planned to be buried there. There was the 3gun salute and then the flag on the coffin was folded and given to me. That was it… He wasn't in pain anymore!

Several months later I went out to visit his grave. I had returned to my car and was reaching for the door handle when I felt a swish past my ear. Then I heard a gunshot. Guess God wasn't ready for me, yet.

I really don't remember much about those few days, during and after the funeral. All the family came, then they all went home. They needed to get home and get on with their lives. That is, all but Vi, she stayed with me through the next week. What a wonderful friend!

Then, I called my office. I told them I wanted and needed to get back to work. Just don't be sympathetic. Sympathy would make me cry.

I remember I did a lot of walking. I would walk through the neighborhood. As I passed a house, I would say to myself "a widow lives in that house, a widow lives in that house, too." I wasn't the only widow. So just get on with your life!

Chapter 11 • Practicing a New Concept

"I have no special talent; I am only passionately curious."
—Albert Einstein

It is true…life alone is different. I won't expound on the difference but it was a new life.

Erv and I loved each other, we cared about each other, we worried about each other, but we didn't do much together. His disability required his life to be sedentary while I would walk, bike, and swim. I didn't enjoy drinking so I didn't accompany him to the American Legion. We did share rides through the car wash and trips to the dumpster. (Yes, we did!) Such was our life together, at that time. But when he was no longer there, it was those warm feelings, when he held me close in his arms or snuggled close in bed, that I missed and still miss. A hug now then would feel good!!

I immersed myself in my work. I wanted to learn more about Myofascial Releases and Cranial Sacral Therapy; more about Trigger Point Therapy, and more about this new disease, Fibromyalgia. I wanted, so much, to be able to help Laurie and the numerous patients who were suffering with the same symptoms as she.

Physical Therapists, like other professionals, were required to take continuing education classes for their CEU Credits. In May, 1984 I attended my first Seminar & Workshop on Myofascial Releases & Cranial Sacral Therapy with John Barnes, in King of Prussia, Pa. What a revelation that was! It opened up a whole new world for me. One in which, just maybe, I could help Laurie.

But first, what is myofascia and what is the cranialsacral theory? Myo is the muscle and fascia is the connective tissue that holds it all together. Visualize: remove all your bones, organs, and nerves. There would still be the myofascia in the shape of you.

The Cranialsacral theory contends that the head bone is directly connected to the toe bone. That what affects one will affect the other. It states that, in addition to our breathing and out pulse there is another rhythm. One in which our body will extend then flex. This movement can be felt by lightly but firmly placing the hands on the cranium and tuning into what one feels. The bones of the cranium will open and close. If there is some glitch in the body, the rhythm in the cranium and the rhythm in the ankles will not be in sync.

I began applying this technique to my patients. I remember one young girl who came in with her Mother. She complained of pain in her right hip & was having trouble walking. On evaluation I found the range of motion in her right hip was limited by pain, especially in abduction. She was unable to lie on her left side and raise the right leg. I began by releasing the myofascia of the internal thigh muscles Then I asked her to, again, raise the right leg. She did and it flew up. She was so surprised! Her Mother cried out and laughed. No one was more surprised than I! We all three enjoyed the amazing success of those Myofascial Releases.

That was the beginning. I realized I had a talent for feeling the tensions in the soft tissue of the body, and that I was able to transfer my energies into that tension to release and stretch it and thus relieve the pain. How can that be? Do you know that at the Baltimore Maryland Science Center there is an exhibit that demonstrates that our bodies have electrical energies? If each hand is placed on separate metal plates the circuit is closed and the electrical energies are measured. Knowing that the human body has electrical energies flowing through it, the medical profession has used electrical currents to help heal fractures and open wounds. Isn't it feasible, then, that these body energies directed into restricted soft tissue will relax and release the tightness?

One patient describes it like this. I quote, "Esther gently strums the fascia until she finds a point of maxim resistance. As she strums, and strokes deeply, she concentrates her energy, her body's electrical force through me—from hand on top through me to hand below me. Granite moves—sometimes the release feels like inches of lengthening, of freedom. Sometimes it feels as if the whole area has dramatically softened, lengthened. There are gradual releases, and swift and sudden exhilarating releases so astounding we both laugh with joy and relief. Almost always after a real release I feel an area of heat where she has concentrated her energy. PS. I myself am capable of many small peripheral releases but not the deep major ones. There is a dimension I cannot achieve myself." (written by Trudy Guthrie)

A quote from another patient: "My first session with Esther was a jolting experience. First, she stood me in front of a fulllength mirror in my underwear. She pointed out how one shoulder was higher than the other. My eyes sought their level (meaning my head was tilted). My pelvis was tilted, my shoulder stooped, and my arms hung down in front like a monkey's, my stomach stuck out. I wanted to crawl under a rock. Then Esther did something and I have never been the same since. I know that is not a very descriptive way to put it, but it isn't an easy thing to describe. It doesn't feel like Esther is doing much at all. She does not apply very much pressure, what she does do, is apply her energies in the correct direction to cause a release. Esther accomplished the first release by digging her fingers into the back of my head, just where the spine joins. I had no idea what to expect. All of a sudden, the tense muscles in my neck, back, and shoulders let go all at once. In a second all the pain I was feeling in the last 7 years was gone. Gone! I felt such a rush of wellbeing and thankfulness that I couldn't handle it emotionally and I began to cry. Esther says this doesn't happen quite so dramatically to everyone. and Boy, is she glad!" (Letter written by Jackie Turnquist)

Now, does that explain it all clearly? Of course not. I can't explain it either. I just know that the Myofascial Releases and Craniosacral techniques work!

I continued to attend John Brane's Seminars and Workshops. Then I wondered if taking Laurie to be treated by John Barnes would help her. She flew home for a week at a time and Marge Loomis and I would drive her to Paoli Pa to be treated by John. I always sat in on the treatments sessions so I could learn more and become more adept with the techniques. One day John said, if I wrote an article for the PT Forum (a physical therapy publication) about my experience using these techniques, I could attend one of his seminars, FREE. I couldn't turn down an offer like that—I wanted to learn more and more!

Lo and behold I became a name! (not really a very big name) I wrote a couple of articles, did some speaking, gave some demonstrations. I really felt important when asked to come to Lexington, Kentucky, to talk about and demonstrate what I did. I was so flattered! Imagine, this little country bumpkin! I was apprehensive. I wasn't a woman of the world. What would I wear, how would I act? I really didn't know what to expect or how to handle it all. BUT I CAN DO THIS! And so, I did. It was all expenses paid. I flew into Lexington airport and was met by the head of the PT department. Isn't it appalling that I can't remember his name or the details of the trip? I guess I did what I was supposed to do.

By the late 1980s BR&L had acquired several more offices and they asked me to speak to a group of their therapists from those offices. It went well. I explained this new technique I was using and its effect on my patients. I was so surprised when they gave me a check for $50. I actually got paid for talking, IMAGINE THAT!! I went right out to Macy's and bought a London Fog all weather coat with zip out lining. Guess what? I'm still wearing it.

To be really honest, I wasn't very good at speaking. In fact, on one occasion when I was speaking, I had everyone's attention and lost my place as I was referring to my notes. I bombed out! It was embarrassing. But mostly, I just bluffed my way through.

You see, the important thing was to get the message of Myofascial Releases and Cranial Sacral Therapy across to other therapists and to get the message out that it helps people with chronic pain. Especially people with Fibromyalgia.

My first article, "The Missing Link in Chronic Pain Relief," was published in 1985 by the Physical Therapy Forum. In 1991 The Advance for Physical Therapist printed my article "Myofascial Releases & the Cranial Sacral Theory Offer Relief to Pain of Fibromyalgia."

I was on a Crusade, one for Fibromyagia! I was seeing more and more patients with this dreadful disease. One such patient was Jackie Turnquist. During her treatment sessions we would talk. We felt it would be helpful if there could be some sort of support group where people suffering this unexplained pain could get together, talk and realize they were not alone. I did not feel adequate to be fully responsible for leading such a group. I visualized some wacky person opening up a can of worms and what would I do, then?

Let me explain about Fibromyalgia. Before 1980 many people, mostly women, would go to their doctor complaining about this pain that wouldn't go away. Numerous tests showed no reason for the pain. Was it all in their head? Some doctors implied as much. Then in 1980 The American Academy of Rheumatologists declared this pain to be real if it met certain criteria. They named it "Fibromyalgia Syndrome." Wow! Now this pain had a name! Still, there was no known cause or treatment for it. But it did help, knowing their condition was not "all in the head."

Jackie was a member of the Southern Maryland Chapter of the Maryland Arthritis Foundation. She came to me with a proposition. That chapter of the would sponsor a Support Group, if Jackie and I would lead it. It was arranged that I should talk to the AF board members and present my case. I did just that. I explained how important it was for these people, who could see no light at the end of their tunnel, to learn that they were not alone. A support group could bring them together to talk about how they are living with the pain. There would be speakers; speaking on pertinent subjects. Perhaps Dr. Teeter or Dr. Mary Michael would speak. They were rheumatologists who sent me patients and were familiar with the situation. We could introduce several periodicals such as the Fibromyalgia Network, which published updated info on FM. It really didn't take much convincing, for, Voila! Our Fibromyalgia Support Group became a reality in the early 1980s. We were pioneers, for there were only one or two other FM groups on the east coast that we knew about.

We had been meeting for a while when we were visited by two women from Washington DC. They wanted to start such a group and wanted to talk to us and see what we did. (That was flattering.) (We were proud.) (Sorry, again, about names and dates.)

The Washington group grew. It set up a board of directors with members who must have known people of importance in congress. They lobbied for Fibromyalgia and were able to get a law passed that put FM on the list for Medical Disability. That was a big help for Laurie.

I was 61 years old when Erv died. Four more years until retirement! Many people look forward to retirement but not I. I was loving my work! I was healthy. Life was good. When 1984 arrived, I decided I would continue to work until I was 70. So, I did all the necessary legal stuff—like visiting the Social Security office and signing papers for my social security benefits. Because Erv had put more into his Social Security, and I was his spouse they had me on his account. Of course, because I was still working, the monthly payment was less.

All was well. I was working. Jackie and I would meet once a week with our FM Support Group, which was very well attended. Sometimes, as many as 60 people were there to hear the speaker and learn more about FM.

Then in 1991 BR&L sold out to a big Physical Therapy consortium, Physical Therapy Associates. I continued working but it was no longer fun; there were restrictions on my time spent with a patient. Maybe I was a bit burned out, too, for in 1993 I retired. My goal of working to age 70 was not achieved.

Retirement meant sleeping late in the morning. Lots of Free Time! I needed more than that. I needed to be needed. Because of my connection to the Arthritis Foundation, through the Support Group, I knew Jan Thompson, the director. She needed a volunteer in her office to do odds and ends of jobs. I was the perfect candidate. Her office was located in the little stucco house on B&A Blvd and The Trail. I didn't have far to go. The times I remember most were the special fund raisers; the Jingle Bell Run every December at Marley Station Mall and the summer run at Quiet Waters Park. The Jingle Bells Run was always early in the morning. It would still be dark and very little traffic when I drove up to Marley Station. The previous week we would have filled the goodie bags with pamphlets on arthritis, etc, and freebee stuff gleaned from local business. There was always excitement in the air. There was registration and handing out the goodie bags and Tshirts. Then there was the race and the winners and the ceremony of giving out the awards. Fond memories.

The "Run" at Quiet Waters Park was fun. One summer, the Olympic Gold Medal winner, Mary Lou Retton, was the guest. You see, she had had a hip joint replacement and was a good representative for the Arthritis Foundation. Her appearance was a drawing card. The participants enjoyed having their pictures taken with her and going home with her signature on something. More fond memories.

There was always the annual Christmas party when the board members would host a party for all the Volunteers. One year, Jan was doing her welcoming thing when she looked at me in a strange way. I wondered if something was wrong. Then she announced that I was the recipient of the Volunteer of the Year Award. The award was like a dual hinged picture with a clock on one side and on the other side was my picture with a plate beneath it, stating the purpose of the award. I was speechless and pleased!

Jan, Jackie and I became fast friends. We celebrated our birthdays together and exchanged Christmas gifts. The day I learned that Laurie had died I had to let the AF office know I would not be at work, that I was flying to Texas. That night, when the doorbell rang I opened it to find Jan, Jackie and Scott, Jackie's husband, standing there. Jackie and Scott had come all the way from Harwood. They had come to be with me and offer me comfort. I will always remember their kindness. But even now as I look back on it, I really didn't want them there. I felt I had to be a good hostess, converse with them, when I just wanted to be alone.

What year did I stop volunteering at the AF? It is all so vague, now. I do know if it happened a few years after Jan was promoted to President of the Maryland Chapter of the Arthritis Foundation. She was so good at her job. I continued to work with her replacements at the Southern Md Branch and all was well. Then National decided to downsize as they called it. I really don't remember, or if I even knew, just what the situation was but Jan was told she no longer had a job there. We were all so very shocked! We couldn't understand it. I was mad. Mad at the Arthritis Foundation. Jan was devastated. I worked another year, but there were changes in the Southern Maryland Office, too, and I wasn't needed any longer.

Jan later moved to North Carolina and I hear from her at Christmas time. Jackie and I still celebrate birthdays and Christmas. Life goes on.

Chapter 12 • Life After 1985

*"You must live in the present, launch yourself on every
wave, find your eternity in each moment. For fools stand
on the island of opportunity and look toward land. There
is no other land, there is no other life but this."*
—*Henry Davis Thoreau*

As I look back at 1985, I can see how The Lord has blessed me in so
many ways. During the months that followed Erv's death my family
and so many friends were with me, supporting me. My children, Vi
Sopko, Marge Loomis, and the people where I worked. Vi insisted
she stay with me for that first week. Bless her heart.

There was the trip to Allen Pond Park
with Marge and Sandy and Eileen and
Daryl and Gerritt.

There the children rode the little
train, watched the ducks on the pond—
one was strange looking and Marge and
I called it a chirkendoose. Actually, a
Muscovy.

There was the day trip with
Marge, to Cunningham Falls,
just north west of Frederick. It
is a lovely place, and if you've
never been there you should go.
Cunningham Falls is a Maryland
State Park located in the Catoctin

Mountains. There is a cascading waterfall, a manmade lake and the remains of an old Iron Furnace.

On the way home we detoured and found an old covered bridge. We dove through it. Frederick County is known for its covered bridges.

On December 14, a new tradition began. The Loomis family came to my house to celebrate Sandy's birthday. We celebrated Christmas too. Good friends sitting around the fire, opening gifts, laughing and joking. It was warm and cozy. It was good!

Then there was Christmas day when all the family was here. Rick, Eileen, Daryl and Gerritt came up from Florida. Laurie and Greg flew in from Texas. Mother was here and even the Kolar's, Marilyn, with Miriam and Meredith, stopped in from Ohio.

A wonderful finale after a few difficult months.

Have I mentioned, I have a wonderful caring son? In June 1986 he moved his family back to Baltimore, MD, about an hour from me. He began working for James Posey & Associates in Baltimore—Engineering contractors.

I never had the joy of babysitting grand babies but now I had the opportunity to spend time with my grandsons! What a Joy that was! I would drive up and get them and bring them down for a night or two. I remember one occasion, when I arrived at their house, I was sooo sleepy. I needed a fiveminute nap. I stretched out on the couch and asked them to wake me in five minutes. They woke me five minutes on the dot.

Often, on these occasions, we would drive to special places—like the Naval Academy, or we would join Marge and Sandy at Allen's pond. Of course, there was always the Cape Arthur Beach, when the weather was warm, or the playground in the school yard in back of my house.

1987

Our winters today just are not what they used to be! We measured 10 inches of snow on the monster the winter going into 1987. My pictures show a lovely winter wonderland! I was healthy and strong then and enjoyed shoveling a path to the street. And, of course, getting out to feed the birds. Lots of birds—cardinals, chickadee, titmouse, nuthatch (the upsidedown bird), 3 different woodpeckers. I remember the little brown creeper—so cute. And the pesky squirrels. The snow under the big hickory tree was black with nut shells.

Mother turned 89 in March. We marveled at how well she was doing. She needed a walker but otherwise she was doing amazingly well.

When spring turned a corner and things started blooming, my friend, Marge, thought it time for a change of scenery. A trip to Chincoteague and Assateague Island, VA. was just the thing. The weather was perfect. We found lodgings at Refuge Lodge, located at the entrance to the park. We rented bicycles, bought some snacks and began touring Assateague Island, famous for its wild ponies. Yes, there were ponies, in fact, we came upon a group of about 6 that were grazing along the path. To our amazement and joy there was a new

foal among them. It was still wobbly on its spindly legs. Some were curious about the baskets on the handlebars of our bikes. They were friendly and we were able to pat them. We were careful, though, for, they were, after all, wild ponies.

Everywhere we looked there was new life. The ducks and geese on the lakes had their babies following them. The little Sika deer were caring for their young. Life was beautiful. I thought to myself, "Next year I must bring Rick and his family here to see and feel the wonders of this new life."

This is as good a time as any to explain about my friendship with Marge Loomis. How did she happen to become such a good friend? Well, it all started back in 1982 when she broke her ankle. (Did I tell you she is my boss's wife?)

I became her Physical Therapist. During her treatments we soon discovered we had much in common and enjoyed the same sense of humor. We began doing things together such as bike riding and swimming. She sat with me when Erv was so sick and dying, and planned outings to keep me going after he died. I will always be grateful for such kindness and thoughtfulness. A true friend, indeed!

Our friendship blossomed. We took more trips together and enjoyed birthdays and holidays together with her family—Wil and Sandy.

Now, Marge & Wil had two children, a son Richard and a daughter Sandy.

Sandy was a Downs Syndrome child, with a hip displacement. She was fortunate to have parents who were wise to that condition. They were strict about her diet to keep her weight down, they were strict about her behavior. She was a lovable little girl. She would always join Marge and me when we went swimming. With her bad hip she had a problem walking but boy she could swim! We would often stop at Friendly's for ice cream afterwards. It was a treat! If it was lunch time, we might order a banana split.

Have you heard of hippotherapy? Relationships with animals are good for people, especially people with handicaps. Being on a horse and connecting with that animal is therapeutic. And so, it was, with Sandy. She was a site to behold! She could really "sit a horse." She has numerous ribbons to prove it—lots of blue, some red and yellow ones. I would sometimes attend her shows. And take pictures, of course.

When Sandy finished high school, she began working at jobs through a vocational service group. Later she became the laundry gal for BR&L. She and I would time our lunch so we could eat together. I often took cottage cheese with pineapple. She noticed this, and on my next birthday she gave me a magnet that said," You can't live on cottage cheese alone." Sandy liked to visit card shops and found this magnet for me. She had a wonderful sense of humor! Yes, she could read greeting cards.

Marge and Wil were concerned for Sandy's future. I joined Marge on several trips to explore future residences for her. (Those are another story.) They finally opted on a home in Northern PA. Martha Lloyd. There Sandy was cared for and could enjoy activities and have a job as well. And, she could continue horseback riding.

I often joined Marge when she made a trip up to visit Sandy. Sandy was a good friend and it was always a happy reunion.

It is sad but as Downs Syndrome people were living longer it became a reality that they would develop dementia. Sandy died in 2009. She was 50. I'm glad I never saw her in her dementia. I want to remember her as I saw her one evening after work at her home. She was, gracefully, descending the stairway singing "here comes "Miss America!" Always that sense of humor!All my fellow BR&L coworkers attended her funeral. Sandy was special and we all love her.

Chapter 13 • Remembering

"Memories are timeless treasures of the heart"
—Unknown

As Daryl and Gerritt were getting older and closer to school age, Rick and Eileen thought they should search for a home in an area where the schools were highly rated. They found such a home in Ellicott City (Howard Co.). The location was good, I guess the price was right, and the house was well built, but the previous owner was a smoker. All the appliances in the kitchen were nicotine yellow. I offered to help Eileen clean the kitchen prior to their moving in, and what a job that was! I will never forget what a time we had scrubbing the inside and outside of the refrigerator.

In August 1987, when they were settled in, Laurie, who was here, and I went up to see this new abode. It was newly painted

and showing off Eileen's unique and lovely decorating colors and designs. She did have a way with colors that would never have occurred to me. But I liked what she did. She was a free spirit.

I spent Thanksgiving with them that year. Eileen's folks, Esther & Ed. were there, too.

Now that I'm old and living in the past, I find it is fun to remember the special times, back when my porch and patio were the place for family fun. There might be a crab feast with the Wheatley's or with Marge and Wil and Sandy Loomis or a celebration of my birthday.

It's fun to remember the quiet evening at Cape Arthur Beach, watching the sun go down; remembering how, each fall, my church, Our Shepherd Lutheran Church, would take a trip to New Windsor, Md. We delivered clothing and quilts to the Lutheran World Relief warehouse. From there they would be trucked to delivery points and then sent to needy countries. I remember on one trip, there was an armed bullet proof vehicle waiting in the warehouse, waiting to be shipped to a wartorn destination. These trucks were needed to protect the delivery people. We always stopped at Bagher's Restaurant and Market for lunch and to buy fresh produce, and homemade pies and other goodies.

It was always a treat. I usually came home with an apple dumpling or a blueberry pie.

There were 3 special occasions that helped 1987 go out with much cheer and good will. Sandy Loomis and her family celebrated her birthday at my house on December 14, and again, a few days later for our annual Christmas gift exchange.

The grand finale was having my Mother and Rick and his Family at my house for Christmas. I found, in the album, a card from Eileen, saying: "to the greatest Motherin law in the world." Wasn't that nice? She was grateful for my help with cleaning up the new home.

That was the year I began celebrating Christmas Day in Maryland, then flying to San Antonio, Texas to celebrate Christmas again with my daughter, Laurie and Greg. How I loved the Christmas season!! I still do.

Gerrit was 6, on February 25, 1988 and we celebrated at his other grandparents' home, (Ed & Esther Moran). Ed had a workshop where his small grandsons delighted in exploring. Ed had them doing all sorts of fun things. I remember Daryl had a microphone and pretended to be a DJ at a radio station.

MOTHER WAS 90 in 1988! Imagine 90! Now, that called for a real celebration! The whole clan came to celebrate. The club room at her apartment was available. There were decorations, and food, and… entertainment. Maurice was the MC. We sort of roasted Mother, sharing stories about her. He introduced Miriam

and Meredith Kolar, who played their flutes, and Daryl did his magic tricks. We showed, on screen, such old slides that were available; pictures of the family. Everyone enjoyed and laughed, at seeing themselves from the past. Ed Moran arrived and took video pictures of everyone and the celebration. Eileen, then, drew a picture: a banner saying "Celebrate 90

years 18981988." Under the banner she drew caricatures of all that were present. I have to tell you; Eileen did an amazing job of characterizing each one. You really could tell who was who.

I always enjoyed going to Texas and being with Laurie and Greg;  spending about 10 days there. I remember, on one of the first trips, she took me sightseeing. We stopped by what looked, to me, like an orchard. I was soon to learn it was no orchard, but a grove of Live Oak trees; short trees, not tall like in Maryland, with heavy branches that spread out as long as the tree is high. Wonders of nature! Beyond those trees was a field of Beautiful Blue Bonnets. Well, we just had to go out there and sit in the middle of that patch of Blue Bonnets. We had to take each other's picture, too. It was fun! Laurie continued, every year, to take her family out to sit in a patch of blue bonnets and take a Blue Bonnet picture. I received a new one every year.

Remember I said I wanted to take Rick and his family to Assateague Island? Well I did just that! Like my trip before, we went in early May when everything was new life. It was Rick, Eileen and Daryl and Gerrit, and me, of course. We stayed at Rustic Lodge, near the bridge to the island. We rented bicycles, Eileen and Gerrit rode a tandem bike, for he was still too small to ride alone. The weather was perfect. We saw the deer, the ponies, the geese, all with their babies and we rode to the lighthouse which is no longer in use. It was fun sharing it all with my family! I wonder if the boys remember.

In September Marge and I drove out to visit Nany. On the way

I insisted we detour from Rt 68 and visit the Casselman River Old Stone Bridge. It still spans a creek but is no longer part of a highway. It now joins the property of a Mennonite Restaurant, Alpine Village,

with historic log cabins, recreated buildings from the golden age of the old National Road. There you can buy the most delicious applesauce bread fresh out of the oven. If you are lucky, it might still be warm. Marge and I were lucky. We took the warm loaf of bread and walked across the Bridge to a little grassed area with a picnic table. We had no utensils, so, just tore it apart and ate it warm. Heavenly!!

I don't remember when I first started watching the Severna Park Fourth of July Parade. (There was a lot of walking so Erv didn't join me.) The parade would gather at Our Shepherd Lutheran Church and the Episcopal Church, on Benfield Rd. It would march down Benfield to Robinson Rd and make a cut through to Old Annapolis Blvd. I would drive over to the Severna Park Shopping Center, park the car, then, find a spot under the trees along the Blvd. The parade marched right by. I always arrived early to get a good place, and I always took a folding chair and something to drink and nibble on.

One year I took my sketch book and tried to draw the jubilant children, sitting on the stone wall across the street. It was a picture worth painting, the children in bright colored Fourth of July clothes, legs dangling over the wall, arms waving the red white and blue flags, their voice high, calling and cheering. It could have been a great picture! I did try to paint it but was disappointed in the result.

In the early days, the 60s and 70s, we always looked forward to seeing the SPHS Band march past with their sharp looking uniforms, their prizewinning marching and delightful marching music. The Grand Marshal was usually a WWI veteran, or some prominent public person riding in an open slickedup convertible. In later years it was a WWII veteran and then a veteran from the more recent wars. Sadly, there has always been a war, but happily there has always been a veteran.

There were lots of floats and open bed trucks with elaborate scenes depicting the theme of that year. I was always amazed at the creative talents that made up those floats. They were sponsored by various communities and organizations, like boy scouts, dancing schools, flower shops, etc. and clubs.

It was always a good parade with several high school bands, (Severna Park High being the best); several Fire Departments, blowing their sirens; bicycles, always a unicycle, little children with tricycles; old cars; horses, with someone walking behind with a pooper scooper. It was just great fun to watch, to wave flags, and cheer!

In later years, the parade changed course, still forming at the 2 churches but coming down Benfield, then Evergreen to McKinsey Rd, turning south on B&AB to Cyprus Creek Rd and finally turning left into Sunrise driveway and going on up to Wood's Church parking lot. Some went on to Ritchie Hwy and the antique cars turned right into a parking lot there.

I changed my watching station several times; first, by the bank building, then along Cypress Creek Rd. I'm not sure where I parked each time. But I had my lightweight folding chair and there were trees along the sidewalk. I had my sun hat and drinks. I would meet friends along the way—always Mary Dill—I would recognize her walk anywhere.

When Rick and Joanne moved to Severna Park, he got a big kick out of watching the parade too and would join me. I am living at Sunrise, now, and have only to walk through the campus to Cyprus Creek Rd and set up my folding chair. The parade passes right by. Rick and my grandchildren (Gerritt, Melanie, Sandy, Vince, Drew) have joined me, too. Guess we all love a parade!

Sadly, the parade isn't what it used to be. There are more vehicles, but, fewer bands and clubs and communities participating, fewer floats, but it is still fun! I wouldn't miss it.

Remember I told you about Erv's buddy Dick Sopko and how they always came to visit in February and in the fall? After Erv's death I wondered if they would still continue to come. They did, and in September 1988 we began the first of many adventurous trips.

Harper's Ferry was our destination. Dick and Vi had driven down from Cleveland and had their car. So, he chose to drive, though later they would fly down and I did the driving. (I liked to drive.)

Harper's Ferry is a town on a mountain side with two rivers converging at its feet. The Potomac comes rushing down from the mountains to the west, while the Susquehanna comes up from the south. They are historically known for their frequent flooding. There is a tourist sign at one building that indicates the high flood mark.

We shopped and climbed the steps to the church. I forget how many steps.

There is a railroad bridge crossing the river and entering a tunnel in the mountain.

An overnight stay in Harper's Ferry, then on to Berkley Springs. That's the town with the special Hot Springs and Spa where wealthy people go to get well. Or so they say. Well, of course, we had to try the Hot Springs Baths and the Massage that goes with it. Dick and Vi thought it was good, but I could have told the masseuse a thing or two. Actually, I thought she was terrible. I thought she was going to push me off the table.

Laurie & Greg Adopt

NOW, I must tell you about the really big news of that year 1988. It was in September that Laurie and Greg unofficially adopted some older children. They felt that Laurie, with her FM, would not be able to do all a newborn baby required. They applied at the Adoption Center and went through all the interviews, home inspections and paperwork. They were finally introduced to a brother and sister and fell in love with them. Mark was 11 and Sandy was 8. They had been in a foster home but were now in a real home. A happy time for all!

I celebrated Christmas three times that year. First, and keeping up tradition the Loomis' came to my house with gifts to exchange and fun and laughter.

Then on Christmas day, Mother, Rick, Eileen, Daryl and Gerrit joined me for a festive exchange of gifts and a Turkey dinner. How can one fully describe the joy of watching your grandsons open their gifts? I had two cardboard boxes, each shaped like a barn and with their names on them. I had filled them with wrapped gifts and I watched as they gleefully emptied the Barn. Every Christmas they looked forward to seeing those Barns under the tree. It was tradition!

The next day I flew to Texas and celebrated Christmas all over again.

This visit was especially exciting for I would be sharing their first Christmas with the soon to become, new Skalla Family.

The necessary trial time passed and in September 1989 we all drove, (yes, moi too.) to Del Rio, TX. I was the babysitter while Laurie and Greg went to the courthouse and attended to all the legalities. While that was going on, the children and I played in the swimming pool and at the museum next door. Later we went back to the courthouse so the children could do their thing. They finalized it with pictures of all the participants. I was included in one final picture. NOW, they were really a family! Greg and Laura Skalla and their two children, Mark and Sandy Skalla. What a happy day! As we were leaving Mark reached across the seat, put his hand on Laurie's shoulder and said "Hi MOM." I had tears in my eyes.

As we left De Rio, Greg decided we should see the Amistad Dam that crosses the Rio Grande river and connects to Mexico. I'm sure they all enjoyed it but it was really exciting for me. There was a dividing line on the road with Mexico's Eagle with Snake on the south side and the US Bald Eagle on the north side. I stood with one foot on each side—one foot in Mexico and one foot on my home land. Once in a lifetime!

I was disappointed and saddened to notice the Rio Grande River was not a river below the dam, but just a trickle, while, on the other side the dam is brimming, a beautiful turquoise. (I can imagine how the folks living below the dam must feel, with only a trickle of water.)

In May 1989, Jackie Turnquist and I drove to Columbus, Ohio, to attend a Fibromyalgia seminar. We drove my car, which had automatic transmission. Jackie was used to driving a stick shift. We took turns driving. We decided to travel by way of Grantsville, Md, and stop at the Mennonite restaurant, Penn Alps, next to the historical Old Stone Bridge. We toured the old buildings that housed artisans, demonstrating their particular craft. Best of all, we bought a hot, just out of the oven, loaf of their famous applesauce bread. Then we walked across the bridge to a little grassy spot with a picnic table and ate the bread. We tore it apart with our hands—it was sooo good!!

We continued on our way, Jackie driving, and started down the steep curvy Cheat Mountain. Jackie was nervous and she wished for her own car with a stickshift. She could throw it into gear and drive safely to the bottom. (This was the mountain where I once did heat up my brakes, but was fortunate to find a turning off spot before reaching the narrow bridge at the bottom,) Anyway, Jackie was a good driver and we made it safely to the bottom.

The seminar was held at the Ramada Hotel along the Olentangy River. We enjoyed a stroll along its banks during breaks. The seminar was informative and encouraging. We were excited to go back to our FMSG and tell about all the new findings. There was still no known cause or cure, just suggestions on helping the pain. Drat it!!!

We stopped in to say hello to my cousins Eddie and Sue Buck who lived in Gahanna, nearby.

Nany died that year. It was October 24th, 1989. She was 95, and still living alone in her little house in Lillian's back yard. Lillian had been caring for her, taking her meals, taking her to doctors and always checking up on her. Dave had kept her old pendulum wall clock wound and running. Her companion was a little black cat, Midnight, that sat and watched TV with her.

Rick and I drove out to the funeral.

When my nephew Ray Miller, son of Alma and Ray Miller, got married May 25, 1990, I drove out to Bay Village and stayed with Lillian and Dave.

The wedding was beautiful, the bride was beautiful. All the Lang Clan was invited. It was really good to see so many relatives and friends. (Old home day.)

The next day Lillian and Dave took me sightseeing. I lived in Cleveland for 12 years but had never visited Lake View Cemetery where President Garfield's resting place and Monument is located. It is an interesting building.

We also visited the Terminal Tower, downtown Cleveland. It was once the tallest building in Ohio. It was the central train Station for the B&O Railroad and other railroad lines. Now, only local trains come in there. It once housed the big department stores such a Higbee and smaller select stores. I would sometimes go there to do Christmas shopping. All that has changed, now.

Another day Alma and Ray drove me down to Amish Country, near Mansfield, OH— one of their favorite things to do. Amish Country—you know—good food, crafts and the World's Largest Coo Coo Clock. Now, that was a sight to behold. It was a chalet type building. You could stand beside it and watch the people come out and go in. Amazing! Of course, we bought goodies, but no crafts.

I couldn't leave Cleveland without seeing Dick and Vi. Now, who better to go with, to try to find our old cottage, Langrila. Would the cottage still be there? We drove through Harpersfield and Mechanicsville, located the covered bridge but had to drive around it on a new bridge. We found the turnoff road that led down to the cottage. That narrow road hadn't changed. When we reached the end of the road, there stood our old cottage— same as always, with its porch, and red trim. Boy! Did that bring back memories— swimming, boating, sitting around in the evenings, watching the fire in the outdoor fireplace. Fond memories!

Chapter 14 • Trip to Poconos

"You and I have memories longer then the road that stretches out ahead"
—Unknown

June 2124, 1990

This account is from my journal of that trip.

It was the Summer Solstice, June 21 when we started out for the Pocono Mountains, a beautiful, warm, sunny day. We got a late start because we both had to work half a day. I, also, had a dental appointment. Marge had to work, take Wil and Sandy to the airport to visit their son in Memphis, and take her dog to the kennel.

It was about 5pm when she picked me up. She was so tired I drove. The traffic was heavy—evening traffic—everyone going home, but no problem. We drove three hours to Frackville, PA, where we found a neat place to eat—Dutch Kitchen, all country deco, with homemade bread and apple butter. We weren't impressed with the food but the bread and apple butter made up for it. (We were both trying to eat "good"; watching the cholesterol.) Dinner was $19 for both of us.

It was getting dark so Marge took the wheel. We drove another 20 miles, to Hazelton, where she had found a "neat" motel— Hamilton Motor Inn. Here, again, the décor was quaint and clean. Room was $44.53 (AARP rates).

June 22. Again, a beautiful, sunny day, temp 88°. We woke up early and were eating breakfast by 7:30am. There was a Bar and Deli next door to the motel that was open for breakfast. So, we had our English Muffin, orange juice and coffee (for me).

We were on the road again, in short order, headed for "Mount Pocono". We had decided to detour and try the Mule Rides into the mountains. It was 10:00 when we found the place, back in the hills. It was quite a sight, with mules wandering loose, grazing on whatever they could find.

We met one of the workers, who was suffering from an auto accident. Well of course, I got into a long discussion about her physical therapy.

We did, finally, mount our mules. Marge's was named Stanly and mine Candy and our guide was Richard. He was very nice and helpful. It really was a fun adventure! Marge changed into culottes and as we mounted, we both laughed at each other—it was our bony knees! A real sight for the picture taken after the ride. The ride took us along a narrow path, over rocks, through bushes, through mud that squished as the mule's feet sank into it. We had to avoid tree trunks, and overhanging branches. We saw a small deer along the meadow edge, and a mule who was wandering loose because he could untie his rope. The path took us up to Knob Hill where we looked out over a beautiful valley, across to the mountain range into NY and NJ. At the end of the ride our pictures were taken—knobby knees and all.

We left the mules behind and continued on to reach our final destination, The Overlook Inn, around noon. We were welcomed and shown to our room in "The Lodge", a separate building from the Inn. The Inn, itself, housed the kitchen, dining room and a lounging room with fireplace—cozy!

June 23, rain was predicted but, so what? We decided to explore the 8 falls at Bushkill Falls. We drove down Rt 447 to Stroudsburg, then headed north up Rt 209 to Bushkill. Bushkill Fall is part of a federally owned park. We bought our tickets $4.50 and $3.75.

There were 3 different paths we could take: a 45 min; a 1½ hour; and a 2½ hour. We started up the 2½ path but got half way and decided to take the shorter one. Even that one took us 2 hours.

 We walked along the water, over some very rocky terrain, in some places, over bridges and catwalks over water. And a hill with 100 steps. The river water rushing, cascading over small rock or huge boulders, over fallen tree trunks. It was awesome!! We did see 7 of the 8 falls, and were duly impressed. The climbs were steep and we often stopped to rest. We took some pictures, though there was limited light in some areas.

These falls reminded me so much of Swallow Falls and Muddy Creek Falls in Garrett County. (nostalgic)

Around 4:30 we were ready to welcome the end of the trail and a cold lemonade. We really were exhausted! But revived enough to shop the souvenir shop.

On returning back at the Lodge we showered and dressed up for dinner at the Inn. Breakfast and dinner are included in the price of the room—$80 a night, each. Marge likes fish so she ordered the Trout, but I had Chicken ambrosia. It was just OK and came with an appetizer, salad, and dessert.

Other guests told of a black bear that visited the garbage cans each morning, and of seeing a 4point buck deer in the back yard of the Inn that evening. Maybe we will see them too, tomorrow.

June 23, awake to rain but a little rain could not deter our high spirits. We were at breakfast at 8:30 enjoying cinnamon flavored popovers, blueberry pancakes, fresh orange juice, and coffee. Ummmm good!! We saw no bear, or deer. As it was still raining, we decided to do indoor things. First stop was Calle's Candy Kitchen, it's their own homemade candy. It was fun browsing but expensive. I did buy fruit slices for Mother and C & C, and fudge for Rick. We browsed several other craft shops, and the Christmas shop. There I bought Christmas mugs for the children. The mugs said "Jesus is the reason for the season," then about the real reason for Christmas.

After lunch the sun came out so we decided to see what Colony Village was all about. It was a disappointment—just a tourist trap. We spent no money and no time there.

That afternoon I laughed at Marge when she told the Inn manager we were in room 10. He insisted she was wrong because there was no room 10. She was so sure until she checked and discovered we were in room 35. All along she had been signing our meal tabs ROOM 10.

We had dinner at the Inn, then, as we were leaving to go back to our room, we saw several deer standing along the side of the driveway. When Marge tried to take a picture of them, they ran off across the driveway into the woods. One was a young buck with just nodes for antlers. The poor fellow's back hind leg was off at the knee. But he coped. He was able to keep up with the others.

We were up early, for we were heading home. We got in a nice walk before breakfast. It was another beautiful day—we had been so blessed with good weather.

Guess what? That morning, the bear came for breakfast too. The kitchen staff said we could see it and took us through the kitchen to the wooden fence with the dumpster behind it. We could see the bear rummaging through the garbage. Marge wanted a closer look to take pictures—I cautioned her to not get too close. That bear was not worried when he saw us, but kept on rummaging. We went back into the dining room where we were seated by a window looking out onto the back lawn. We soon saw the bear, carrying a ½ gallon mayonnaise jar in his jaws, come lumbering across the lawn. Just as he came to the woods, and almost in front of our window, he sat down and began reaching into the jar, with first one paw then the other and licking it. He must have entertained us for about 10 minutes, before he took the jar in his jaw and lumbered off into the woods. (I love to tell that story.) It was a grand finale for a grand weekend!

I was at the wheel when we headed home. It was very frustrating when we got to the Philadelphia bypass. I couldn't understand the Pennsylvania road signs. Marge to the rescue. She was from Philadelphia and was familiar with the area so got me safely around that city and home. I will always be grateful to Marge for planning such a wonderful trip. We really had a good time.

Chapter 15 • Camping
at Deep Creek Lake

"Birthdays are good for you.
The more you have the longer you live."
—Unknown

1990

Birthdays ending in the big "0" always need to be celebrated. When Miriam was 70, she and Maurice came up to Glenn's to celebrate. It was the 4th of July (her birthday was June 20, 1990.) We gathered on G & G's deck, Mother, Moi, C & C, Rick and his family.

We played Bocce ball and had a good time just being together. By the way, Gail is a very good cook.

 The next morning, M & M and Moi headed to Cumberland to take the scenic train ride on the Western Maryland Railroad. It ran day trips, through the mountains to Frostburg, Md. and back. I took the lead, in my red Sable, for in his camper it was tricky merging into Rt 100, then Maurice took the lead. His camper rides high and I could follow him easily, but, more importantly, he knows the way.

We made good time, for in less than 3 hours we reached Cumberland and the train station. We boarded the train with its

139

vintage cars. They were newly painted, with ornate wainscoting on the walls. The new upholstery was accented with colors of cream and soft green. There were other cars but they were not as fancy as ours. There were not many cars for Maurice tried to take a picture of it as we rounded "Horseshoe Curve" but it wasn't long enough.

The trip was a bit disappointing, for all we could see on either side were trees. It certainly was the mountains, alright. When we reached Frostburg, we had lunch, shopped, and admired the scenery there. We watched the train as it was turned on the turntable to head back. Then, we boarded the train for the return trip. It was a four hour trip, and we enjoyed it!

On the road again, destination Grantsville and Casselman Inn. You ask, what's so special about Casselman Inn? Route 40 was the Old National Pike that connected our nation from the east to the west and much traveled. Casselman Inn was strategically placed along that road. Can you imagine the stories it could tell? It is of brick structure— bricks handmade and burnt on the land. A fireplace in each room furnished heat and cooking facilities for the original building. It has been upgraded with the presentday comforts but still maintained the historic atmosphere.

The Inn had small rooms and limited space for extra bathrooms. (Sorry, no room with bath.) A bathroom was shared by three rooms or five rooms. Getting fussy in my old age, I fused about sharing with five, but settled with three.

That settled, it was still early, we walked down the hill to Casselman Bridge, and then crossed over to Penn Alps. You know about them from my trips with Jackie and with Marge. This trip though, we did take time to visit the tiny log cabins where local artists demonstrate pottery making, weaving, woodworking, etc. Of course, we had to stop in at Penn Alps for some of their applesauce bread and go to the tables under the bridge to eat it while it was warm.

After dinner we ambled through the rooms, admiring all the antique furniture and the old pictures. The sitting room was not available in the evenings because the lights wouldn't turn on. It was still light and lovely out so we walked up Main Street and discovered The Army Band from Fort Meade was giving an outdoor concert in the park. We only stayed a short time, for it had gotten colder—we had no jackets. So, we returned to the Inn for our dessert—homemade pie and ice cream. Now, I ask you, "who could ask for a better way to end a lovely day?"

The next morning, after a breakfast of delicious buckwheat cakes, maple syrup, and sausage, we headed out, destination Deep Creek Lake State Park. We stopped along the way at several mountain overlooks to admire the panoramic view, looking down on green pastures, trickling streams, and in the distance more hills and forest. It was a photographer's dream.

This was a trial run, for M & M wanted me to join them on some of their camping trips. We needed to know if their little camper would work with three bodies, eating and sleeping. Well, it was hilarious!! No problem finding a campsite, but when it was time for bed, we had to unload the camper and put everything in my red Sable otherwise animals would get into the food.

But first, we left the camper at the park and took my car to shop for food for supper and ice, then to visit some of Auntie's old friends. The Shrocks, of course, Jane Wagner, and Anna Virginia. They were all pleased and surprised to see us and all seemed to be doing well.

That evening dinner was delicious as Miriam can make a feast out of nothing. Maurice built a fire and we roasted turkey dogs, had chopped veggies and later roasted marshmallows to eat with graham crackers. Maurice played his harmonica and Miriam I hummed. There was a moon, too!!

Then it was time for bed and we had to figure how we would sleep. I wish I had the words to really explain what a hysterically funny situation it was. We folded up the table and made a small bed for Miriam and I.

Then we watched as Maurice struggled to hike himself up into the overhead compartment. Needless to say, we giggled and laughed at him but when Miriam and I tried to get comfortable in this little bed, trying not to fall out, we all laughed. We laughed so hard our sides ached. It truly was a very comical situation.

The next morning, we reloaded the camper, and had breakfast at Point View, on the lake. Maurice and Miriam were on their way to spend 3 weeks with their daughter, Marilyn, in Ohio. I headed back east, stopping once at the rest stop between Hagerstown and Frederick, for relief and to enjoy the remainder of the applesauce bread. It was an easy trip and I was home by 2:00. That was really fun! I hoped we could take more trips together. We did.

Chapter 16 • Disney World

"Laughter is timeless Imagination has no age And dreams are forever."
—*Walt Disney*

When Nany died in October 1989, her inheritance to Erv went to his children, Rick and Laurie. Good hearted Laurie felt badly that I didn't get any. So, in August 1990, when she and Greg made plans to take their children to Disney World, she invited me to go along – all expenses paid. I couldn't turn down an offer like that.

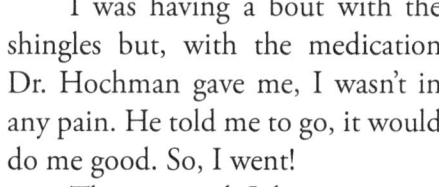

I was having a bout with the shingles but, with the medication Dr. Hochman gave me, I wasn't in any pain. He told me to go, it would do me good. So, I went!

They invited Lila to go too, but she paid her own expenses. We flew together to Orlando where we met Laurie and family, boarded a mini van and with Greg behind the wheel we began our Disney World adventure.

Laurie was a great travel agent and had each day (5 of them) carefully planned. As I read my journal, I really can't recall all those places we visited or the lines in which we stood, or the food we ate at different exotic restaurants. As I recall we were rushing from place to place. However, I do vividly recall the smiles, the laughter, the excitement and utter joy Mark and Sandy were experiencing. It was fun watching them, and watching Laurie and Greg with the children.

On departure day the Skalla family boarded a plane back to San Antonio and Lila and I headed back to Baltimore. We had an hour or so to wait for the plane, and since it was lunch time, we bought something to eat. My sandwich didn't set well. I knew I was going to pass out so laid down on the floor between the seats. Lila, the nurse, bless her heart, took charge. The funny thing was, I could hear everything that was going on and that was said but I couldn't lift a finger. I was taken to the hospital, had a nap, and was fine. A bit disoriented but fine. And very embarrassed!! What a dumb thing!! Somehow, we made plane connections and got back home safely. Lila was a jewel!

The Skalla family made it home without incident.

Good memories

My life has just been one adventure after another. I'm so glad I wrote journals and kept photo albums to help me remember. Now you must remember, I was working, and honestly, I can't remember if it was full time or part time. (I've told you about my work.) Somehow, I found time to enjoy lots of adventures, too.

There was the weekend Vi and her friend, Fran, flew down for a long weekend. We were headed to Rehoboth Beach for some sightseeing and ocean enjoyment.

My grandson, Daryl, was getting his Eagle Scout award that night, at the Boy Scout camp near Aberdeen, Md. I had never missed any of their special Scouting affairs and didn't want to miss this really special one. Aberdeen was on the way to Rehoboth. So, plans were made. We would get a motel room in Aberdeen; Rick would come get us and drive us to the affair. (Remember, I don't drive after dark.)

That afternoon as we were driving up I 95, cruising along nicely, I suddenly see up ahead this truck that had a small gardentractor on it and some loose tires. Then I see a loose tire come flying off the truck right at me. Oh my gosh, what to do? There isn't time to do anything....... It flies over us and bounces on the road being us. Vi saw it coming, too, and we both heaved a sigh of relief! Thank you, Lord!!

We arrived at our motel in Aberdeen, then Rick picked us up to take us to Broad Creek Boy Scout camp, where the ceremony was to take place. Daryl was to receive his Eagle Scout Award. It was a campfire ceremony and was very impressive and enjoyable. We were all so very proud of him.

The next day we continued on to Rehoboth. I repeat, what is it about the ocean that is so appealing, soothing, awesome, magical? Having a balcony room that faces the ocean and sitting there listening to the rushing waves.....what more can I say...

The good weather was with us until we headed home. We had reached Cambridge when the skies opened up. It was hairy driving for a bit, could hardly see the car ahead. Debated pulling over but decided it was better to just keep going. Finally, we drove out of it and decided to stop for lunch.

I can't remember where we stopped but it was a fast food place. We picked up our order and were sitting at a booth when some guy came and sat down next to Fran. He was trying to be cute. I was upset and asked him to leave, but Vi and Fran were leery of him. They were afraid if we made him angry, he would wait for us outside and do us harm. I'm a country bumpkin and not used to city dangers

so was not worried, but we couldn't leave until they were sure he had driven away. We made it home safely with stories to tell.

Christmas!! Christmas, that year, 1990, was wonderful! One evening, a few days before Christmas, Marge and Sandy stopped in. We sat on the

145

floor in front of the fire and exchanged gifts, laughed a lot and had a good time. It was Christmas and we were celebrating together.

Best of all, was having Laurie and her family home for a week. Now, we really celebrated! They had to spend a few days with Lila, but that was OK.

Do you know, Mark and Sandy had never seen snow? I believe it snowed just for them. The day they were returning from the Baltimore Science Center it started to snow. And it snowed. We brought the sled down from the attic, put plastic bags over their shoes and pants and took the children up to the front school yard. There was a steep bank they could sled down. Gee! You should have seen them. Such fun! Well, first I had to show them how it was done. Later, we played fox and geese in the back yard, and made snow angels.

There were 13 for Christmas dinner that year. Laurie and family, Rick & family, Lila, Barb & Terri, my Mother and Moi. Later, Charlie and Kim, Glen & Gail, Maurice and Miriam came. They played "break the pinata" out in the back yard. Everyone wanted to meet this new addition to our Clan.

Laurie's birthday on March 11, 1991 was a good enough excuse to fly to San Antonio to see them all, (and maybe do something to relieve Laurie's pain. I was never successful, but maybe having her Mother there gave her some comfort. She just took a lot of pain pills.)

Laurie had a big box full of clippings of interesting and fun places to go. This trip, she decided we should go to Wonder World. It really was a wonder when we walked into the antigravity house and saw everything at an angle. I still don't know how they did that. When we looked in a mirror, we looked lopsided, but it was kinda neat, you felt off balance. Then we walked through a newly discovered cave. It was recently discovered after an earthquake. Interesting! Mother Nature at work.

April 1991: Trip to Longboat Key, Florida

Remember way back, when I told you about my friend, Mary Mosser. We were at Fort Custer, together, training to be Physical Therapists, and we roomed together when we worked at the VA hospital outside of Chicago.

Well, she married the boyfriend, Don Randa, the guy she visited every day when we lived in Berwyn. They set up housekeeping in Burr Ridge, outside of Chicago. Don had inherited a percentage of the Cicero Newspaper and was financially secure (?!!?) We kept in touch at Christmas but when she developed FM, she wanted to learn more and came to one of the seminars here, where I was speaking. Our friendship blossomed and they invited me to visit them at their condo in Long Boat Key, Florida. Wow! What an opportunity!!

It was a marvelous new adventure!!

It was in April, 1991. I flew to Sarasota, Florida, where Mary and Don met me.

During the ride to their home, they pointed out interesting places we could later see; the summer home of Ringling Brothers Circus and the Pelican Man Bird Sanctuary. The latter perched on a little inlet where we crossed the bridge that took us across Sarasota Bay, from the mainland, to Longboat Key Island. The island is situated about midway along the Gulf (west) coast

of Florida. It is one of the Barrier Islands which are separated from the mainland by Sarasota Bay.

It was a new world for me, with palm trees, bougainvillea, and oleander bushes everywhere. The sun was shining and it was April—with temperatures ideal for swimming and sun bathing. I was in Paradise!!

Their condo was within a large Condo Complex. They were on the ground floor facing the blue waters of the Gulf of Mexico. We could step out their patio door and a few yards to the left we could be at the pool area with palm trees, and tropical plants and, then to the right we could take a path that led us to steps over the sand berm to the beach and the Gulf (& the pelicans).

You ask, what is a berm? It is like a sand dune, and manmade. It is probably 30' deep and rises maybe 15 20' high. It follows the Gulf Coast as a protection against the ocean. It is planted with grasses and other salt water resistant plants.

There are wooden steps that we traverse to get to the beach. Not far.

What did we do during those glorious days? Well, first of all we donned bathing suits and sun gear, (sun hats, sunscreen and folding chairs) and went to the beach. I was fascinated by the pelicans. Did you know they fly, following the direction the fish are swimming, then they suddenly switch direction and swoop down to let the fish swim into their big bills. Ingenious, uh? I had a book, but didn't read much—too interested in watching the pelicans.

After soaking in the sun, we cooled off in the pool, then went out for a leisurely dinner where we sat and watched the sun as it sank below the Gulf of Mexico. What a life!!

The days were full! There was always the time on the beach with the pelicans then the cooling off at the pool and we talked! And we talked! There were many years to recall. We relived the old years at Fort Custer and the VA hospital. It was fun! We laughed a lot.

There was an evening when we went out to dinner then attended a Sondheim concert. I had always enjoyed his music.

Life was so leisurely—I was up earlier than them, so would take a walk on the beach, then breakfast would be ½ grapefruit or juice, toast and coffee.

One afternoon we visited the Summer Home of the Ringling Brothers Circus.

It had once been a magnificent place but had become run down. I honestly don't remember much about it.

We ended the day with a trip to the beach, a swim in the pool, and then dinner at a little place right on the Gulf. We sat on the porch, for I wanted to watch the pelicans resting on the bulkheads, but when it started to rain, they closed the curtains so we wouldn't get wet. So much for pelican watching. We did get to the Pelican Man's Bird Sanctuary. Now that is quite a story. It goes like this: Mr. Shields was told by his doctor that he needed to get away from the stress of his job. So, he bought a little house on a piece of land that sat on the Saratoga

Bay near the bridge that crosses to Longboat Key. One morning he goes out to find a wounded pelican. He brings it in and settles it in his bathtub. He took care of the wound but he could see it would never be able to live on its own so he built a pen for it. He named it George and it became a member of the family.

Word got around and soon people were bringing other birds for his care. Some birds just seemed to know he could help them, for he would often find another pelican or a sea gull perched on the pen hoping for help. He finally set up a "surgery" where a Veterinarian was on call. He set up a company with a board of directors to see that it would continue after his death. (Don was on that board.) He built a boardwalk along the pens and one could buy a board by way of contributing. Of course, I had to buy a board.

One day Mary said she wanted me to see Lido Key Island beach where there were lots of interesting shells. Rain was predicted but that did not deter us. We went prepared, we thought. But when it started raining our short jackets were not enough. Mary and I got soaked. The weather was warm but we didn't mind. Don was dry under his big golf umbrella. We did find some nice shells, and I brought some special one's home.

On the way back to the condo, we decided to stop at a special ice cream place they liked. Mary said she would go in and asked Don for some money. He reached in his pocket and pulled out a rolledup wad of money with a rubber band around it. He peeled off a bill and gave it to Mary. Well, I couldn't let that go without a comment, so said, "Gee, look at that, I've never seen a roll of money, before. That's impressive." Then he reaches in the other pocket and pulls out another wad.

Don was a rather short man and he liked to impress people. I liked him in spite of it. All good times must come to an end for I finally had to fly home. It was wonderful, those few days! Mary and I had so much in common. We enjoyed the same things, and we had so much to talk about. I hoped I would be invited again.

Chapter 17 • 50th Class Reunion

*"You wouldn't worry so much about what other people
think of you, if you realized how seldom they do."*
—*Eleanor Roosevelt*

That May, 1991, BR&L moved from Murray Ave. to Defense Highway, into one of the Conti Buildings. We occupied the entire second floor. (It was a 2 story building.) We had expanded and now had a large gym, and separate treatment rooms, a break room with microwave, etc, a laundry, office for the bosses, and a reception room at one end where the elevator ascended. And…. I had my very own corner room where I applied my techniques of MFR and Cranial Sacral therapy to patients with FM or other chronic pain problems. I had quite a following!

Memorial Day was enjoyed at the Moran's cottage on Stony Creek. Rick and his family were there, and I was invited, too. We swam, ate, played games—I won a cup. I was in good company and really enjoyed the day.

What a life I lived! Full of happy, enjoyable times, and working at a job I really enjoyed!

Then June arrived. I had earlier received an announcement of my 50th high school reunion. I had not attended any previous reunions, and didn't feel any real ties to that time in my life, but 50 was a milestone and I should not miss it. I should go.

My good friend, Marge, encouraged me and offered to make the trip with me. I knew it would be a fun trip and full of laughter if she was with me, even if the reunion turned out to be a disappointment.

On the way, of course, we stopped at the Old Stone Bridge, and Penn Alps to have the warm applesauce bread.

The reunion was to be held at Will othe Wisp on Deep Creek Lake. It was the first Hotel & Restaurant built on the Lake. I can remember it, way back, when I was a child. It now has cottages, for rent, on the grounds to the side of it, but Marge and I got a room in the hotel. There was an indoor pool as well as the beach, for swimming and sunbathing, and a marina.

We settled in; all the while Marge is pumping me about the people from my past. I said, "there was one person I would like to see." "And, who's that," she said. "Well, you see," I said, "there was this boy, John, I dated through high school and I wondered and sort of hoped he would be here." I broke off with him while in PT school. Dad had said he had brought his wife to meet my Mother & Dad, though, I can't imagine why. I knew he had moved to California so

couldn't imagine him coming from there just for a reunion. And I didn't know if I would even recognize him.

As we wandered through the place, curious about all that was there. Marge kept asking, "Do you see him, is that him?" When we came to the indoor pool there was a man with a woman in the pool. I looked, but wasn't sure. Was it he? Would I know him? Marge is really enjoying this! Her comments were not helpful.

Finally, it was time for the big event. (Marge chose not to join us.) I did remember a lot of my old classmates, but there was no John. I don't remember what was for dinner. I remember they read off names of those who had died.

Then pictures of the whole class were taken and we all took candid photos of ourselves with friends. It was nice and I'm glad Marge talked me into going.

Chapter 18 • Trip to Michigan

"In every walk with nature one receives far more than he seeks."
—John Muir

Camping with M & M, June 28 to July 21, 1991

It was 1991 that Maurice, Miriam and I took off on our second camping adventure. I remember that Maurice was a wonderful leader, Miriam was a wonderful cook and I had a wonderful time following them!

We had learned from our trip to Deep Creek Lake State Park, that I needed to have my own car, and camping equipment. So, with my Red Sable car, a small tent, a folding army camp cot, a folding camp stool, and battery lights, I joined my brother and sister inlaw for a twoweek vacation exploring the state of Michigan.

Now, you must realize, this was before cell phones and we needed some way of communicating while on the road. We each bought a CB. Neat, uh? Their call name was M & M and I was Red Sable—"Calling M & M, this is Red Sable, come in!" Sounds good don't you think? It was fun.

 **On June 27**, M & M arrived at my house. We had each purchased a CB set, and needed to do a trial run test around the community. The testing proved to be a lot of fun and the CBs worked fine.

The next morning, I finished packing, checking to be sure I had  all my essentials. Tent to live in. check; cot for sleeping, check; camp stool for sitting, check; lamp for seeing, check; suitcase of clothes, check; cooler for food, check; CB for talking, check; coats for any weather, check. M & M were already waiting and anxious to get on the road.

We were off, on a grand adventure! It was an easy trip to our first stop, the farm in Ohio, where their daughter, Marilyn, lived. We drove west through Fredrick and Hagerstown, stopping at the rest stations, then up to Breezewood and the Pa Turnpike. Turning off the turnpike at Rt 70 into Ohio, we stopped for gas and at Wendy's, for lunch. We arrived at Marilyn's farm in time for supper.

Maurice had to show me the farm. There was much to see.  Tom was raising sheep, the girls, Miriam and Meredith, each had a horse, there were ducks and chickens, cats, and 2 dogs. It was a large farm with a lot of wooded areas with maple trees. A garden and a creek feeding into a pond. It was really quite lovely, but a lot of work for them. They were also music directors for churches. The girls were busy, doing well in school and winning ribbons in horse shows.

We were warmly welcomed and generously fed. I was very tired so hit the sack early. M & M were glad to have time to visit with their daughter. Ohio is so far away from eastern shore Md.

I slept well and was awake at 7:00. Marilyn was having some back pain so we did some exercises that might help. Miriam joined in with the stretches. It was good for all of us.

After a breakfast of delicious waffles with their own maple syrup, we said our thank you and were on the road again. Destination, Ann Arbor Michigan, to visit an old friend from home, Betty Hancock.

We stopped, at a Mc Donald's, outside Marion, Oh. for lunch. Later when we turned in at a gas station to ask for directions, I got out of the car to hear the directions too, and before I knew it, Maurice was back in the camper, taking off and I didn't know where he went.

That was when the CB proved its worth. "Calling M & M this is Red Sable come in". We connected and got back together. I really fussed at him, tho. My big brother taking off and leaving without me. (just like when we were kids).

We did enjoy talking through the CB. We would comment on things we saw as we were driving.

My alma mater, Bowling Green St. Univ. was not far out of our way. My sorority was to have a sort of reunion on the 29th. I would be on my way home, and would be able to stop and attend the get together. It would be fun! The timing was perfect! We detoured to BGSU, so I could call a sorority sister, Betty Canfield. She would make a motel reservation for the 29th.

We arrived at Betty's around 5:30. Betty was an old friend from home who, after a divorce, had moved to Ann Arbor, to be with her sister. We greeted each other with a hug and I introduced Maurice and Miriam. Her daughter, Nancy, stopped by in time for dinner. Wow—grilled steak, baked potatoes and a delicious dessert. She gave me the recipe—strawberries with cool whip, topped with meringue.

Betty was up early the next morning ready to fry us eggs and bacon for breakfast, but we had to decline, for we were on a strict no fat diet. Bless her, she was gracious, and offered us cantaloupe, rolls and coffee.

After breakfast, we left the camper, for we would be back to spend another night there. Then we headed for Dearborn and the Ford Museum. It was always easier to get around with the smaller vehicle.

There was much to see at the Ford Museum. There was a solar powered automobile, built by engineering students at the University of Michigan. They had proved its reliability and speed when racing from Florida to Ann Arbor. They came in 3rd, winning a ribbon and a place in the museum the Moon Vehicle.

There were a lot of train engines, some were huge! There was a bicycle built for nine, an antique bathtub, old kitchen appliances, and old farm equipment.

We were exhausted by 3:00 and decided to head back to Betty's, but first we wanted to get her something; a box of candy, to show our appreciation. After driving around, we ended up at a mall where we bought a box of Whitman's Samplers. (Our dad used to always give our mother Whitman's Samplers.)

Betty served us a delicious chicken supper and Nancy joined us, bringing a lemon dessert she had made. We were all sated and needed a walk. Betty showed us the park with swimming pool, and a cobbledstone house.

We ended a lovely day by sitting on her deck, talking and reminiscing. I expressed my pleasure that she was happy in her lovely home and in such a nice community. I was very happy for her.

It was sunny but colder when we woke up at 6:00 the next morning. We had driven through some muddy roads at Marilyn's yesterday, so before breakfast, I took advantage of parking in Betty's driveway and washed my car.

After a healthy breakfast, and words of thanks and praise for her kind and generous hospitality, we took our leave.

Heading north again we came upon the little Bavarian town of Frankenmuth. It was a delightful town with typical Bavarian architecture. Many folks were dressed in typical attire, and eating places served the typical food. We walked around the town, then drove through the covered bridge, saw the dam and the mill, but the wheel wasn't working.

We had lunch of bratwurst and sauerkraut, at the Koffey House at the Bavarian Inn and enjoyed listening to a woman singing and playing polka music on an accordion.

We were in time to watch the little people in the Glockenspiel Tower come out and dance around to the music and hear the clock ring the time.

From Google: *The Bavarian Inn Glockenspiel Tower houses a magnificent 35bell carillon, a beautiful figurine movement and an illuminated clock, all imported from Germany! The sound of the Glockenspiel can be heard for miles around Frankenmuth with lively German and American tunes and hymns. The sound originates from a 50foot bell tower where installation of specially cast carillon bells and figurework*  *for the Pied Piper of Hamelin was completed in October, 1967. Before striking the hour, and on each quarter hour, the clock sounds the 5bell Westminster chime. At Noon, 3 p.m., 6 p.m., and 9 p.m. each day the Bavarian Inn Glockenspiel plays several selections which are immediately followed by figurine movement depicting the legend of the Pied Piper of Hamelin.*

Leaving Frankenmuth, we continued north to our first campsite. I was feeling some apprehension, for this would be my first night in the tent and it was supposed to rain.

Maurice was an old hand at camping and had planned ahead. We were to camp at Tawas State Park, on the shores of Lake Huron. As we entered the park, we purchased passes for Michigan State Parks. $15 per car for entrance into park, plus $9 per night, for a campsite. We planned on being there two nights.

The campgrounds were crowded, but we were lucky to find site #118, next to the toilets, and showers. Whew. I breathed a sigh of relief!

Outside the toilets, we saw a nest of chipmunks; Maurice counted 8 little ones. Miriam and I took pictures.

No rain yet, so we set up camp. I pitched my tent, set up the camp cot, with sleeping bag etc., folding chair, and was all set for the night. In the meantime, Maurice and Miriam were organizing the camper for cooking and getting ready for supper. It was delicious! Chicken and rice from Betty's and fresh broccoli and potatoes. Dessert was angelfood cake from Marilyn with canned peaches.

We cleaned up and were going to walk to the beach but it started to sprinkle.

So, we stayed in the camper, looking at maps and brochures, and planned for the next day.

This was quite an adventure. It was 10:00 and time for bed and I needed to brush my teeth, wash up, and take my eyes out. (I forgot to tell you I was wearing contact lenses and had to remove them every night and put them back in every morning. When they were out my vision was not so good.) I went off to the rustic facilities. It was just sprinkling so all went well.

The night proved to be interesting. I had a small camp stool and my cooler to put stuff on. You see, I failed to zip the door tight and the floor was wet. However, once I was settled into the sleeping bag, adjusted myself to the cot and ignored the wind, I slept like a rock. Something woke me at 5:00 but I went back to sleep.

It was 6:30, **July 2nd**. I washed up and put in my eyes, then decided I had better pack up everything and get it into the car before it started to rain again. Maurice helped me to take down the tent and spread it out over a picnic table to dry. Miriam had breakfast ready. We were eating well. It was homemade bread from Frankenmuth, coffee and pecan twirls.

It was cloudy and windy but not raining. The tent had dried, so I rolled it into a neat 8" by 24" cylinder, ready for another cozy night. Since this park was situated on the shores of Lake Huron, we wanted to find the beach and the lighthouse. We drove to the beach and parked near a trail that led to the Tawas Point Lighthouse. It sat on a point of land that extended out between Lake Huron on the east and Tawas Bay on the west. We took the trail and walked out to the lighthouse. It was a lovely lighthouse! *(I have a thing about lighthouses. They fascinate me. I guess it is because they are a life line in a storm.)*

It was the canoe ride down the Au Sable river that always comes to mind when I think about this Michigan trip. We had found a campsite in Old Orchard Park on the Au Sable River, near the town of Oscoda. We set up camp but spent the day being lazy. We needed a lazy day after much siteseeing and driving.

We took a leisurely walk along the river, finding a sandy swimming area, steep banks, lots of boats, and the river water so beautifully clear. After supper, we drove into Oscoda to see what was there. Our coolers were full so we had no need to shop and drove back to camp.

Observations… We noticed, as we were driving through southern Michigan, that the land was relatively flat, like the Eastern Shore of Md. The wildlife was seagulls, black squirrels, chipmunks. Maurice saw a Baltimore Oriole and a Pee Wee sang to us.

161

Michigan, like Maryland, is the US in miniature. It has the shorelines of Lake Michigan on the west, Lake Huron on the east, and a touch of Lake Superior on the north west. There are sandy beaches, and high sand dunes, and tourism. It has the plateau with farms, fields, orchards that yield cherries, peaches and apples. In the Upper Peninsula you'll find the mountains.

Comments... We have had two days of camping and now have a sort of routine. Miriam does the cooking, with Maurice and I helping with the preparations. We eat lunch while on the road, bringing with us any leftovers, or sometimes we'll find a picnic table and eat there. Breakfast and supper are always eaten in the camper, or by a fire. Breakfast is usually cereal, bread and jelly, and coffee.

At night, I take my eyes out in the camper, but put them back in in the wash hose in the morning.

M & M gave me a little battery lamp, so I was able to read some at night. The battery lights the smaller bulb but an electric hookup will light the bigger bulb. If the campsite has an electric hookup for the trailer, I can plug into that, otherwise I use the battery.

The camper is equipped with all the necessary kitchen electric appliances, a table that converts to a bed, and a toilet. That item makes it necessary for Maurice to regularly visit the dumpsite, where he can dump and rinse everything.

After completing all our chores, we left the camper and headed out to explore.

This was a forested land and Lumber was king. There was a monument to the Lumbermen. It was a large sculpture of 3 lumbermen with their tools of trade. The story of the lumbermen was told on bulletin boards around the monument. They told about the dangers and hardships of lumbering; Of how the men spent the winter cutting the trees, hauling them to the river banks. In spring they would wait for the early thaw and drive the logs down the river to a holding station. On the way there would be log jams, rapids to cross and other obstacles. It was dangerous for the men who were riding the logs and could be crushed if they missstepped.

One bulletin Board told of how lumbering created thousands of acres of cutover land where the topsoil washed away by rain, and the woody debris remaining on the ground fueled raging summer fires. Times have changed and forests are  being replanted with white pine, red pine, jackpine and tamarack.

We were climbing a bit when we passed the Eagle Nest overlook and on to the Largo Springs Overlook. It was the Springs and the River that we wanted to see. We pulled into the parking area. The view from the overlook was lovely. Taking the trail down to the springs, we counted 297 steps that curved around before reaching the river. I don't remember the Springs. But you know what? There were 297 steps going back up!

Our curiosity led us to drive around in search of 6 hydroelectric dams on the Au Sable River. We found 4, Loud Pond, Five Channels Pond, Cooke Pond, and Foote Pond. We covered a lot of territory and enjoyed the scenery along the way, but were hungry when it was lunch time. There was a small picnic area along Rollaway Road that was following the river. We stopped and Miriam brought out the subs we had purchased at a little roadside grocery store. It was delicious! Why does everything taste better, when out on a picnic? Especially if one can watch the blue water of the Au Sable river flowing by.

The tranquility of that moment passed, when we heard thunder. Hoping to beat the storm, we drove into Oscoda to do some needed grocery shopping. We were back in camp when the storm struck with loud thunder and bright lightning. It continued on and off but cleared up around 6:00. We had hoped to have a fire and cook hot dogs, but it was too wet, so ate inside the camper. We'll save the campfire for another night.

It was still light and too early for bed so we walked around the campsite, looking at all the trailers and tents and talking to people. Campers are always friendly.

Maurice and Miriam are bird watchers. They are constantly on the lookout for a new bird. Their excitement was contagious when they spied a Blackbilled Coo Coo.

July 4. As we were leaving the camp, we saw a long line of cars waiting for campers to leave so they could go in. It was, afterall, the 4th of July weekend!

The Au Sable River zigzags it way south easterly. It seemed we were always crossing it one way or another as we searched for a camp sit and a canoe rental.

We settled in at a small State Park with primitive camping.

After pitching camp, we watched some tubers floating down the river. Tubing and canoeing seemed to be popular sports here. The river current was flowing fairly swift, but no white water, just fast. All the attributes for good tubing and canoeing.

I was ready for a nap and was soon dead to the world. An hour and a half later I awoke. I really must have been tired. It was raining again!!?? Oh well we'll just drive around and find that canoe rental for tomorrow morning.

On returning to camp, I discovered the rain had changed direction and was raining into my tent. I was dry inside the camper with M & M, until bedtime. The rain had eased when and I went to my tent. It was saturated, but my bed was dry. I did sleep well, in spite of it all.

The next morning, I was awake early and anxious to get everything packed and, in the car, so I could take the tent down and spread it out to dry.

We were canoeing down the Au Sable River by 8 o'clock. Finally! For $18 we could float for 2 ½ hours to another rental station, where they would drive us back to our car.

When I recall this trip to Michigan, it is this canoe ride down the Au Sable River that comes to mind with such pleasure. Just picture this! It is early morning. The sun is bright and warm. We are the only canoe on the river. It is quiet, except for the birds waking up and talking. M & M are whispering, that's our red canoe quietly, identifying the bird calls. I am in my glory, feeling it, absorbing it.

Maurice belongs to several camping groups. As a member he is eligible for a discount and passes to certain parks and campsites. He tries to take advantage of these whenever possible. I think most of the camps we were in were discounted, and when we first started, we had purchased season passes to Michigan State Parks.

July 5. Hartwick Pines State Forest was our next stop It was afternoon when we arrived, and were fortunate to get the last campsite. It was a primitive setting and our campsite was far from the johns. Oh dear! I hoped I wouldn't have to go potty during the night.

After setting up camp we walked to the Interpretive Center, then followed a trail to one of the few Virgin Forests still in existence in the US, and the largest White Pine tree. Wish I had taken a picture of it.

Supper was cold chicken, cauliflower, salad and fresh cherries. We had stopped at a roadside stand and bought several quart baskets. Cherry season! One must enjoy them while one can! We ate out on a picnic table and Maurice built a cozy fire. He played his harmonica and we roasted marshmallows for smores. We sang some too. I can carry a tune, if a tune is being played—otherwise, shut your ears!

It was a comfortable ending for a busy day.

Saturday, July 6. It had rained during the night but cleared up. We had been having a lot of rain but not so much that we hadn't been able to do and see what we wanted.

Did I mention that Miriam is a very good cook? Breakfast that morning was pancakes and chicken sausages, and coffee. Miriam couldn't find the syrup but the jelly tasted just as good.

The sky was clear by 11:00 when we took the 3mile Au Sable Foot trail. The river was just a narrow stream where the trail crossed the western branch of the river. The trail led us through a forest of pine, spruce, and fir. Fern was prolific, lots of different mosses, crows' foot, huckleberries (reminders of picking huckleberries at Lake Shore40 as a kid.)

I heard but didn't see any birds but Maurice identified many of the calls. I did recognize the chickadee, but not the oven bird or the prothonotary.

Two and a half hours later, we were back at camp, ready for lunch and a nap.

I was bushed! Miriam served us lettuce, cottage cheese with pineapple, regular cheese and ice tea. She was just amazing!

I napped some but really needed a shower. No shower, no electricity, no running water. Remember, this is a primitive camp. My journal reads that I somehow managed a sponge bath.

It was a lazy afternoon. I read some, Maurice walked over to the lake but said there wasn't much to see. We needed ice so drove into Grayling and found some at the sports store. There was a stand on the corner selling fresh cherries. The lady liked Maurice and gave him two for the price of one.

Maurice built a fire and we roasted hot dogs. There was cauliflower and baked beans, too. The roasted marshmallows were a sweet ending to another enjoyable day.

There was no rain to disturb the night but the neighbors were having a noisy party.

There was loud talking and it sounded like pounding and cracking nuts. I hoped they enjoyed the nuts.

Sunday, July 7, I was up at 6:00 as usual. I washed and put my eyes in, then pulled up stakes for we were moving on. We had a quick breakfast then headed north on Rt 75, for the Upper Peninsula.

The land we were driving through was rolling hills, like the hills around Frederick and Hagerstown. Michigan is a lovely state, with plains, and rolling hills, inland water and rivers, the Great Lakes bordering her. There is farm land, orchards of cherries, apples, apricots, and forests of pines and hardwood trees.

Mill Creek Park was not a camping park, but was more a museum, with a store and a film showing the history of the area. There was a simulated logging camp where Maurice helped a man, dressed in the costume of the 1700's, demonstrate a sawpit. There was a sawmill run by water pouring down a sluice to a flutter wheel and a tub wheel. Funny, how history is much more fun when you are older and can see it in person.

However, it would have been more enjoyable if I hadn't been hurting from a blister on my big toe. So be it!!??

We headed north through Mackinac City to Wilderness State Park. I Remember it being near and sort of under the Mackinac Bridge, right on the lake and near Fort Mackinac. We hadn't yet crossed to the Upper Peninsula.

It was a nice campsite near the showers and toilets. I was always grateful for that. We set up camp, had a quick supper of roasted hot dogs, and delicious beets, Miriam had canned. We really were eating well.

It was still early, so after we cleaned up, we drove to the beach. It was a sandy beach with pretty pebbles, and seagulls flying over. We drove around a bit, stopping at another shore area where we saw a couple of swans and, through binoculars could see the Mackinac Bridge. Exciting!

It was Sunday, so when we returned to camp. We ended the day with a short devotional and a prayer, thanking the Lord for his amazing creation and for our safe and enjoyable journey.

Monday July 8. I was awakened by something stirring around, outside my tent. I finally got the courage to go to the bathroom but saw nothing outside. It was not until 7:00 when I got up and showered and washed my hair, that I discovered a rotten potato that Miriam had thrown out. It had attracted a racoon or something, but apparently it didn't like rotten potatoes either.

I was getting excited now, for we were approaching the confluence of Lake Michigan and Lake Huron. Did you know Lake Superior flows into Lake Michigan via the St Mary River, then Lake Michigan, in turn, flows into Lake Huron? It is east of the Continental Divide and the water flows east. Interesting!

Fort Mackinac is sort of under and to the west of the Mackinac Bridge, which connects Lower Michigan and the Upper Peninsula. The bridge crosses the Straits of Mackinac where Lake Michigan and Lake Huron meet.

M & M wanted to tour the Fort but I was nursing a sore toe, so watched a movie about the fort, instead. It has a long history.

From Google: *The British built the fort during the American Revolutionary War to control the strategic Straits of Mackinac between Lake Michigan and Lake Huron, and by extension the fur trade on the Great Lakes. The British did not relinquish the fort until fifteen years after American independence.*

Fort Mackinac later became the scene of two strategic battles for control of the Great Lakes during the War of 1812. During most of the 19th century, it served as an outpost of the United States Army. Closed in 1895, the fort has been adapted as a museum on the grounds of Mackinac Island State Park.

At the fort, we stood, and looked out over Lake Michigan. The water was very clear, and blue. A heavy wind was roughing up whitecaps. The sandy beach was covered with pebbles. It was a pretty picture.

After lunch, we crossed the bridge ($1.50 toll) onto the Upper Peninsula.

We stopped at the little town of Saint Ignace, just across the bridge, and on the shores of Lake Huron. It serves as the gateway to the UP. It is one of two ports with ferry service to Mackinac Island and the only mainland city accessible from the island by snowmobile when Lake Huron is frozen.

We had been on the road for over a week now, and it was time to find laundromat and wash clothes. Miriam was an old hand at this and showed me the ropes.

The laundromat was located right on the shore with a view of the lake and the Island. We paid our $1.25 for a load of wash and $.25 to dry. While the clothes were washing and drying, we wandered around, enjoying the lovely view over the Lake and Mackinac Island. We saw the ferry, some kind of air propelled boat that sprayed up a mighty stream of water as it traveled, carrying passengers over to the Island.

The tourism of Mackinac Island was of no interest to us. We were nature lovers and sought the wilderness. The brochures we had perused during the evenings gave flowing accounts of the four falls at Tahquamenon State Park. We would go there.

It was supper time and 67 miles later, when we pulled into a nice campsite at Tahquamenon State Park. I'm trying to remember how we cooked turkey burgers, and fresh green beans over a fire, for my journal says we did. Miriam must have had some

kind of grill over the fire, on which to set the pans. Whatever...it was delicious, with cookies and cherries to top it off.

Hooray! It didn't rain last night! It had gotten colder and I was glad I had put the extra pad under my sleeping bag. Leaving my socks on had been a good idea, too.

Only had to get up once during the night and was glad we were near the toilets. I really don't mind this inconvenience. It is part of camping and I was having fun! We had no set itinerary, so could veer off the beaten track any time we chose.

Since we were camped near the Lower Tahquamenon Falls, our hike that morning began there. The trail led us through woods and up 116 steps to an overlook. We discovered the river wound around an island creating five small falls. Climbing 97 more steps we reached another lookout point at the Upper Falls. These falls drop more than 50' and are more than 200' wide.

The river water is amber in color due to the tannins from the local trees.

Lunch is often a big meal and supper the leftovers. So, it was knockwurst and sauerkraut at the concession stand near the Lower Falls. With potato chips and a soda. It was $2.90 each. I don't remember what the mistake was but, because the server had goofed, he would only take $2.00.

It was just midday and there was more to see. The Visitors Center at the Upper Falls would give us a different perspective of the falls. So, we pulled stakes and headed there. The building was interesting. It was built in the Amish fashion with big beaus held together with pegs. Maurice climbed on top of the camper to get a better picture of it. He wanted to show it to Tom, his soninlaw, who was working with an Amish man, selling such buildings. It was, indeed, an interesting building.

The trail, this time, had us descending the steps. (Of course, we had to climb them when we returned: 116 + 97). It was like retracing our steps of the morning but on this trail, we could see how the Lower Falls circled the island and we could see four falls. There were boats to row out to the Island, but we chose not to do so.

It was time to move on. Destination for camping, that night, **July 10**, was Picture Rocks National Lakeshore, on Lake Superior. Maurice was always the leader. He always knew the way and I could follow the bigger camper. Did I say he always knew the way? Wrong. He got all mixed up, took a wrong turn, had to backtrack, and we found ourselves on a gravely, dirt road. Maurice's camper was kicking up dirt and dust behind and I was driving through it. Thank you, big brother!

We were searching for campgrounds at Picture Rocks National Lakeshore. We finally reached Grand Marias, located a campsite and set up camp. It was late, 8:30. We were tired and in need of sustenance. Miriam came to the rescue, with a stew of ground turkey, green peppers, canned tomatoes, and noodles.

(I just have to tell about our meals, for it was amazing how Miriam could magically cook up a delicious meal.)

Wednesday, July 10. When I went to bed last night, I was anticipating rain. There had been showers off and on during the day and we had chased black clouds, but there had been no rain during the night. I slept well and was up, as usual, at 6:00.

We pulled up stakes to be ready when we returned, left the camper, and driving my Red Sable, headed for the Lake Superior shores. We parked and walked along the sandy beach, picking up pretty stones. We had heard there were agates to be found on that beach, but we had no idea what an agate looked like. The stones were all pretty and of many different colors, sizes and shapes. Some were multicolored, and of different substance. I picked up a couple of hands full to take home to Eileen and Sandy. They each have rock tumblers and could polish these stones and make them beautiful.

When we returned to camp, a neighbor camper showed us his collections of stones. He pointed to an agate. They all looked alike. It is still a mystery. Guess I should google agates. *(Google: If the rocky exterior of the stone is broken or worn away, check for banding.)* Oh well…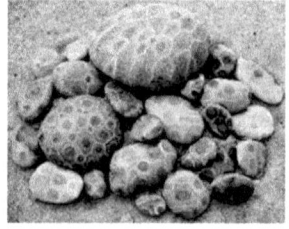

The Sable Dunes were spectacular. Hard to describe. They were on a cliff; sand piled 300' above the water, with humps and hollows covered with vegetation. I took some pictures but couldn't get a good perspective of the awesomeness of it all.

We drove back to camp, picked up the camper, then stopped at a Grill and had a bowl of very good soup for lunch.

Well-fortified now, we continued west to Munising Falls. At the visitors center we were greeted by an older man and woman who were volunteer guides. (They did this during the summer, for fun.) She was an expert on wildflowers, and pointed out some rare species. We descended 97 steps to the bottom of the Falls. We could see the falls as it cascaded over an outcropping of stone. Our guides pointed out the space behind the falls, and we followed as they walked under the falls. I wanted a picture but Maurice said it was too dark. I took one anyway, with my flash. *Haha, it came out fine, so there! That's Miriam in hat.*

We thanked our guides for their gracious and informative tour and were on our way again. We had perused the brochures of Lake Superior rock formations alone the shoreline, and wanted, very much, to see them. We were not disappointed, for we saw not only Picture Rocks but the Miner Castle formation. The castle seemed to be looking into the distance, with two stone lookout towers.

Where we were standing on the beach, we could see a long extension of land projecting out into Lake Superior. It was in the distance, but we could see the rocky cliff and at the very end there appeared to be a formation of a head. Even with a zoom, it was too far away for a good picture.

It was all very beautiful in a photography sort of way and awesome. Another of God's amazing creations.

Having picked up the camper, we headed to Hiawatha National Forest campgrounds. We located a nice campsite, and I set about setting up my tent for the night, while Miriam, with Maurice's help, cooked up some delicious veggies for supper.

After a walk around the camp, and talking to other campers, (M & M loved to meet other campers, hear their stories, and maybe learn of other interesting places) we hit the sack at 10:30.

During the night the temperature dropped to 40°. With socks on and an extra blanket, I slept like a bug in a rug.

July 11. We were up at 7:00, had a quick breakfast, then pulled stakes and headed for

Porcupine St Park. At Marquette, we filled the gas tanks, (expensive$1.20 a gal), and had lunch at Pizza Hut.

When we reached the city of Evelyn, Miriam spied a little place called "Mom's". She picked up the CB and said, "Red Sable, how about some ice cream?" "Oh Yes! perfect, we need a break", I answered back. We pulled into Mom's parking lot, went inside and leisurely enjoyed ice cream and a drink. You see, being able to follow

your heart, to turn off the beaten track and go where new adventures beckons, that's the life!

At Silver City, we replenished our larder, then drove on to Porcupine Mountain Wilderness State Park. We were directed to

Union Bay Camp area, right on the Lake of the Clouds. There were no trees. It was very open, but there was something new, a picnic table. How nice!

We met the people in the site behind us, and guess what? They collect agates! We were soon learning more about that stone. They showed us bags of stones and explained that they were striped, sort of opalescent, and brownish. Perhaps we will know what to look for the next time we walk the shores of Lake Superior.

It was no surprise when it began raining again; a very light sprinkle. Not enough to deter us from checking out the beach. The shoreline was not sandy, with pebbles, but was covered with huge slabs of slate, some broken, smaller and brownish in color. Very interesting.

It had stopped sprinkling, so we sat at the picnic table, eating a leisurely supper of left overs and planning tomorrow's itinerary.

Friday July 12. There had been a gentle rain during the night, but it cleared some, as we packed up to move on. I was following M & M. as we headed to Presque Island. We were still in the forest of Porcupine Mountain.

Finding a parking area, we left our wheels and took to the scenic trail that led to Lake of the Clouds. We could look down and see that the lake flows into the

narrow Carp River, winding through a marshy, swampy valley, and out to Lake Superior.

Back on wheels again we drove around the base of Porcupine Mountain, to a path that led us up 19' to the summit. The view from there was disappointing, just one mountain range after another. It did give us a panoramic view of the vast wilderness that was Porcupine Mountain.

We drove to Presque Island and found a parking lot with a picnic area, where we enjoyed cheese and crackers, peanut butter and crackers, tho I'm not much for peanut butter, and carrot strips. Maurice fed a friendly chipmunk.

The trail to the waterfalls proved to be rewarding. There were wooden steps and walkways, from one waterfall to another, with lookout platforms along the way. The trail followed the Presque River, which eventually flows into Lake Superior. The river has strong currents and occasional rapids and three main falls.

The trail led us across a suspension bridge. You know, those wiggly things on wires? I was brave!

After finding several camps with no vacancies, we were finally admitted to the Curry Municipal Camp grounds in Ironwood. This would be our last campsite. It was supper time, and we were hungry and tired. After setting up camp, we drove to Country Kitchen for a good turkey dinner with appledumpling alamode for dessert. That was just what we needed! We didn't need the hard rain that followed.

We sat in the restaurant for a half hour or so, until it slacked down

some. The streets were flooded. When we got back to camp, we sat in the car, reading about the towns we would be passing through, on our way home.

The tent floor was wet around the edges, but the cot was dry.

Saturday July 13. Needless to say, it had been a restless night... the heavy rain, truck traffic on the road next to the camp, and a cup of caffeine for supper. It was inevitable!

After all that rain last night, today was a beautiful, sunny day.

I packed my gear but spread the tent across a table to dry while we walked across the road to a little restaurant for breakfast. Pancakes with syrup, and coffee. Umm.

We left the camper and drove to Little Girl Point where the beaches were said to have agates. Here was my last chance to find an agate. I couldn't let it alone. I was soon down on my knees looking for pretty stones that might be an agate. *(I brought all my stones home and had the girls polish them, but if there was an agate among them I never recognized it. So be it!)*

We picked up the camper, drove to a Country Kitchen for lunch (not so good!), filled the tanks with gas and we headed east. At Rt 64, M&M left me. They were continuing on to spend another week camping. I needed to get home and back to work.

I would spend the next week seeing the sights of western Michigan. The camping fun had ended. My first night was at the Northern Host Motel Inn, ($29+tx) in Ironwo. Still in the UP.

The Inn was clean and modern. Ah luxury! A hot tub bath, a nap and supper at Big Boys, but I was too tired to eat. Back in my room I called Laurie and watched some TV.

Sunday July 14. Slept later than usual. It was a beautiful day! Had a coffee and a roll at the motel then was on the road by 8:30. As I was leaving Ironwood, I passed an incredible statue. It was a 50' high

statue of the Indian, Hiawatha. It is said to be the tallest Indian in the world. I believe it.

I drove through Escanaba, stopping at McDonald's for an English Muffin and another coffee.

I was still in the Upper Peninsula and driving east along the scenic shoreline of Lake Michigan. It was a delightful drive! I saw three hawks gliding with the air currents. There was yellow clover growing along the roadside, and sadly a spread of burned forest. At Manistique a small red lighthouse stood out bright against the blue water. It was noon, when I crossed the Mackinac Bridge. I was now in Lower Michigan again and it was time to gas up. I stopped at the station just across the bridge. There was a small store next door that sold hot dogs and lemonade. That seemed like a good lunch, I liked hot dogs. It was not to be…. the hot dog and lemonade were lousy! You can't win 'em all!?

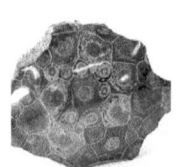

Petoskey was my next stop. This city is named after the state stone, which isn't really a stone but a fossilized coral. As I drove along the lakeshore, I was reminded of Bay Ridge on the Chesapeake Bay. The street bordered the lake with big beautiful homes on the land side, with a view of the lake. I stopped at an overlook and had an iced tea.

On to Charlevoix, a beautiful town on the water, with a draw-bridge and petunias planted along the streets. When I saw a souvenir shop, I pulled to the curb and went in. I wanted to buy something with the Petoskey stone. Of all things, I bought a pill box, and some stones for Sandy and Eileen.

I was in no hurry. I would just take the time and have fun, walking the streets, and window shopping, before driving on to Traverse City. Traverse City was not far from the Dunes so decided to continue on, arriving at Empire around 4:45. Empire was sort of the jumping off place for the Dunes. I drove to the visitor's center for the Sleeping bear Dunes, where I watched a slide presentation and received instruction to lodging for the night, in Empire.

I don't remember the name of the motel, but it was small and clean and had a ceiling fan. However, there was no bolt on the door. It needed to be secured some way. Of course, a chair under the door knob would work. I slept soundly.

Monday, July 15. It was 6:00 and a beautiful sunny day, when I opened my eyes the next morning. A nice long walk would be a good way to start the day. There was no one else up. It was quiet and peaceful.

Finished packing and storing it in the Sable, then went to Joe's Friendy Bar for a breakfast of French toast and coffee. Nothing was open, so just drove around for an hour, enjoying the scenery.

At 9:00 I entered the Sleeping Bear Dunes Trail. There is a story here about a mother bear with 2 cubs. They had been living on the western side of Lake Michigan when a forest fire drove them to the lake. The mother bear, with the cubs following, began swimming across to the other side. Mother bear reached land but the cubs did not. She is sleeping there, still waiting for her cubs.

I encountered a doe with 2 fawns and, later, a single fawn. I stopped at various overlooks and took a lot of pictures. There were other tourists who were willing to snap my picture, and I snapped theirs.

The dunes are indescribable. I stood at the top of one, where the sand had built up over a telephone pole and only the top was showing. As I stood at the top looking down sidewise I could see how very steep it was. We were cautioned not to try a climb down to the water. There would be no way to climb back up. The dunes were really amazing mountains of sand. The view from the top of the dune, looking out at Lake Michigan, was beautiful! I was happy! What a marvel is our God, as he shapes our world.

Time to get back on the road. Heading south, thinking Battle Creek and Fort Custer weren't far out of way, I would just detour in that direction. Finding Battle Creek was no problem, but after a few wrong turns I drove into Fort Custer. I had spent a year there learning to be a Physical Therapist, and met my hubby there. I drove through the camp, it was busy, and I think I found my old barrack but not sure. So much for old memories. I was to spend the night at my friend, Betty Hancock's home and needed to get back on the road. Route 94 took me through the business part of Battle Creek and past the Train Depot. This brought up more memories of traveling from Hines VA hospital to see Erv at the Battle Creek hospital when he had to have his leg amputated. I made the trip every weekend.

Betty and Nancy were waiting for me, when I arrived in Ann Arbor. It was dinner time and they insisted on taking me out for Chinese. Honest, I hadn't planned it that way.

I like Chinese but poor Nancy became ill and we took her home. Betty and I spent the rest of the evening talking. I did call Lilian and Dave to confirm I would be arriving there on the 17th.

Tuesday, July 16. There was so much rain while camping and now the days are sunny and beautiful. Who's to figure?!!

Awoke at 8:00 to another suny, beautiful day. Breakfast with Betty then we drove Mamcy to work. Her car was in the shop.

Ann Arbor was an interesting college town and I was delighted to have a guide to show me around. There was the new campus of The University of Michigan, and there was the old downtown campus, where we went into the old Law School Library building. It was an impressive building with ornate wood paneling and beautiful stained glass windows.

We drove to a little park where a couple were canoeing. A peaceful setting.

Then it was time to pick up daughter, Susan, at the airport. She was a flight attendant.

We all spent an enjoyable evening catting up old times. Susan and Nancy grew up with my daughter, Laurie. More memories of good times.

Wednesday, July 17. Can you believe? Yes, another sunny beautiful day. Breakfast with Betty of cantaloupe (She sure knows how to pick a good cantaloupe). There was the toast, jelly and coffee too.

8 o'clock. Cleveland, here I come! I skirted around Toledo and connected with the Ohio Turnpike, going east, arriving at the Sopko's in time for lunch. My timing was perfect!

Vi was waiting for me with a surprise. Their daughters, Mary Beth and Abbie were there, with their children. It was so good to see them all! They stayed for lunch, then left. After Vi and I cleared up, my wonderful friend, Vi filled a tub with hot, bubbly water and told me to luxuriate in a hot bath for as long as I wished. Ah Bliss!

Dick arrived home around 5:00 and they treated me to dinner at Castle Arms. I was really enjoying this life! After dinner, it was show time. They enjoyed seeing, on the map, the route we traveled, and I showed them my "Pretty Stones". They didn't know any more about agates than I did, but thought the stones pretty.

It had been an exciting day and I was ready for bed, when we called it a night.

Thursday, July 18. It was another sunny, hot day, but the area needed rain. All the lawns were drying up and the farmers were complaining.

The three of us had breakfast at Perkins, a favorite Ohio breakfast shop. That boasted about having the best omelets and pancakes. I heartily agree after cleaning up a plate of veggie omelet and blueberry pancakes.

Dick drove us to see Mary Beth's new home. She wanted to show it off to me.

It was lovely, and told her she had decorated it beautifully, with children in mind. Her children were so cute.

Dick drove us back home then went to work. I gathered up my things, and left to see Alma and Ray. I thought I knew the way, but became confused and had to stop, find a phone and call Alma for directions.

It was show and tell again. I told them about my travels and displayed my pretty stones. Ray was really interested in the stones.

He inspected each one, noting the colors and shapes. It was good, seeing them and visiting for a bit. But I did need to get going for, Lillian and Dave were expecting me.

Getting to Bay Village was no problem. I had been given good directions, and the traffic was not bad on the freeway. Lillian And Dave lived about an hour away so I arrived around 4:30. (Too early for dinner!!??) Alma and Lillian were my sistersin law, but they always felt close like sisters. Lillian and I were especially close, and always enjoyed being together. This visit was no exception. We sat and chatted until Dave got home.

Lillian is such a good cook and dinner that evening was excellent. We sat and talked, I showed them my stones and related stories about my trip, then Lillian and I went for a short walk. This was another thing we both enjoyed doing.

(Every time we visited the Ohio folks we stayed with Lilian and Dave, and everytime she and I would take a walk)

Friday, July 19. It was hot and dry this morning. Everything dying of thirst. I had slept well and was up at 8:30 but was still sleepy after breakfast and went back to bed. An hour later I was awake and feeling fine, ready for adventures with Lillian. We donned bathing suits and drove to the Bay Village Beach, my first and only time to swim in Lake Erie. It was lovely. There were 2 lifeguards; lots of people swimming and lounging on the beach.

We had lunch at a Pizza Hut, and bought fresh corn at a roadside stand. We picked up her two grandchildren, Amanda and Marck and visited the small Nature Center near the beach. There were live turtles, snakes, frogs, fish and snails; a black fox, an albino racoon, 2 skunks, and a turkey buzzard. Mack enjoyed it all but Amanda alternated between being a pest and being fun.

I was the guest of honor and all the Brueggemann's (Mrs B, Gary and Lori, and kids, Diane) were invited for a cookout dinner. Alma and Ray showed up later. It was too much. I was bushed and bed time was welcome.

Saturday July 20. It was another travel day. I was headed to Bowling Green State University to join a reunion of old sorority roommates. After stopping for directions I arrived at Betty's house. My old roommates as well as several other sorority sisters were there. It was a fine reunion, but I couldn't stay long.

Once on the Ohio Turnpike east I was on the lookout for exit 11, in search of a motel. The first 3 looked strange. Drove on to Brecksville and found a motel, $29+tx. They had only one room available. It was 8 o'clock, so I took it. It was clean but old,

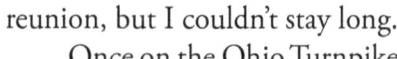

poorly furnished and with a noisy air conditioner, one tiny lamp to light the room and a TV. There was a bolt on the door and I slept well.

Sunday July 21. I was up early and soon out on the Turnpike headed home. It felt good, being on the last lap of a wonderful adventure. The speed limit was 65, but I had set my cruise control to 72. There was no traffic going in either direction so I was sailing along, happy as a lark. Then I saw this patrol car coming up from the other direction in the west bound lanes. I put my foot on the bake and slowed to 65.

When he was level with me he crossed the median strip and turned on his siren. When I pulled over and stopped he pulled up beside me and said, "Ma'am I saw you were exceeding the speed limit but I noticed you braked and slowed down. I guess you weren't aware at first that you were speeding. I'll just give you a warning to stay with in the speed limit." For once, I didn't utter a word. Then he said, "Ma'am I'll see that you get out on the road safely." We were the only two cars to be seen. There was no other car on the road. I said, "Thank you" and drove on.

I did get home safely. When I told Rick about the policeman, he said, "If it had been me, he would have thrown the book at me." I guess being a little old lady has its advantages.

Chapter 19 • Living a good life!

"Someone said, that God gives us memories so
that we might have roses in December."
—*J. M. Barrie*

Life was good, though I still missed Erv. I would find myself suddenly weeping at something so trivial. That was out of character for me, but so be it. I had my children, I had my work, I had my friends and my church. One couldn't ask for more than that. I was truly blessed!

There was the Labor Day Crab Feast at the Moran's cottage when we ate crabs, swam and took a boat ride out to the Key Bridge. Ed proudly demonstrated his new Depth Sounder. He was always keen on new gadgets that delighted his grandsons.

I took the boys to visit the Goddard Space Center. There they pretended to be an astronaut, sitting at the controls and simulating landing on the moon. We all three enjoyed that.

The Maryland Synodical Women of the ELCA held a Weekend Women's Retreat at Sandy Cove Retreat Center, located on a peninsula between the Elk River and the North East River. The view is fantastic!

Joann Jernigan and I attended, along with others from our church. I'm ashamed to admit I can't remember what the retreat was

all about. There must have been a theme, some Bible study, and church services. I do remember I was thrilled when all the women's voices joined together to sing songs of praise to the Lord.

During some free time, Joann and I explored the Light House in Elk Neck St Park, and shopped in the town of North East. When I travel, I always buy postcards to send to my grandchildren.

When it was all over and we headed home, Joann chose to return via Rt 213 south. It's on the eastern side of the Bay where we would pass through Chesapeake City and cross on the bridge over the C & D Canal. The canal was built to connect the upper Chesapeake Bay with the Delaware River (thus, the C & D canal).

Our country and Maryland are not old according to European standards, but we do have our own history that stimulates my interest and curiosity. We stopped and had lunch at Schaeferi Canal House restaurant on the north side of the canal, and explored a bit, then drove over the bridge to the south side. After exploring a bit there, I thought to myself, "this would be a fun day trip with Dick & Vi when they come."

When Dick & Vi came, we did take the trip to Chesapeake City and Canal City. We did more exploring, visiting the museum and I finally got the lowdown on the history of the canal.

Before the Canal was built, ships had to move down the Delaware River, around the southern tip of Eastern Shore, Va., and up the Bay to Baltimore. Now, they had only the 14milelong canal to navigate. There were four locks to raise or lower the level of the water.

The canal was a boon for cargo ships as well as passenger ships and pleasure boats. The economics of the situation was well worth the time and money spent on constructing the canal and installing the locks. Over the years the canal & locks have been enlarged and upgraded 4 times.

On October 2, 1991 a Fibromyalgia seminar was scheduled in Arlington, Texas. I wanted to go—I needed to go and while in Texas, I would visit Laurie & family. I would get CEU credits for this, so was able to take off work. I hoped this seminar would provide some knowledge of the cause and possibly a cure for this dreadful disease. Alas, that was not to be. It was disappointing, but encouraging to know so many medical professionals were searching for these elusive answers.

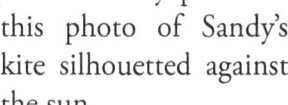

Although I was disappointed, being with the Skalla family was a treat. We attended a musical concert where Sandy was a sheep. We went kite flying at a nearby park. I'm very proud of this photo of Sandy's kite silhouetted against the sun.

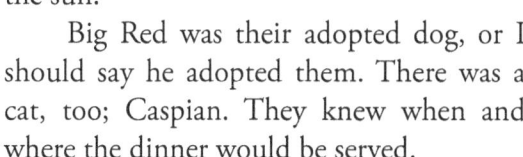

Big Red was their adopted dog, or I should say he adopted them. There was a cat, too; Caspian. They knew when and where the dinner would be served.

During my stay, I would do some MFR and some leg and arm pulls and unwinding. These techniques always gave my patients some relief, why not my own daughter. I always returned home feeling I hadn't helped her. I knew she hurt. She popped a lot of pain pills. But she was always upbeat and good natured.

Trip to Boston

One must never give up. One must always have hope. It was hope that kept me attending talks, seminars and updates of fibromyalgia. This time it was a weekend in Boston; "An Update on Fibromyalgia" was to be presented by the Society for Rheumatic Diseases. Dr. Wolfe and Dr. Carson were to speak. I knew them from the papers they had written. Again, the meetings proved to be disappointing, but I did enjoy the adventure of seeing Boston.

Plenty of history in Boston! However, for a naive country girl finding her way around a city with trams, etc, can be a bit unnerving. I was interested in "The Freedom Trail." Not knowing much about it, I took a subway to downtown and started walking from there. I did find signs along the way that stated the historical significance of each one. But, as I got closer to the waterfront, the neighborhood seemed a bit rough. I was alone and I was afraid to go any farther. So, I headed back looking for the subway to take me back to the hotel. Not an easy task.

The entrances to the subways were not easy to detect and I had trouble finding one. Finally, I found my way back to my hotel. Whew, I was glad to be back in familiar territory. Now as I think back on that walk, I should have taken a tour, I really didn't know where I was going or what I was doing. I was young and thought "I can do this." It isn't always wise to be so independent.

The Christmas season is always special and Christmas 1991 was special too. Marge and Sandy Loomis came with gifts, fun and laughter. We oohed and aahed as we opened gifts, then toasted each other with hot cider.

On Christmas day, Rick and Eileen, Daryl and Gerritt came to my house. Now how could I be any happier? Impossible!

New Year's Eve was at the Wheatley's. When Mother could no longer live alone, her family discussed what would be best and decided that she would be happy living with the Wheatley's, where Charlotte would be home all day. I was still working and Maurice and Miriam were living too far away.

I should explain about Mother. She had been living at the Watergate Apartments in Eastport, near Annapolis for 10 years. I had been her, sort of, caregiver. I would take her shopping, and to doctor's appointments. She had designated me her Power of Attorney.

She had been doing her own cooking, but Laura Fix came every week to clean. Mother always looked forward to cleaning day for Laura had become more than a cleaning lady. Laura was a good friend! She would clean, then stay and visit. Sometimes I would want to do something for Mother and she would say, "don't worry, Laura will fix it."

Mother was a special lady. I remember on one occasion she had a doctor's appointment. We were running late and I kept telling her to walk faster.

She drove me nuts for she would slowly pick up her walker, set it down ahead of her, then step into it. When we reached the car, I noticed she seemed tired. I said, "Mother are you OK?" She replied, "I didn't sleep very well last night." I felt so guilty for rushing her. "Oh Mother, I'm so sorry for fussing at you." Her response was, "that's Ok, I just shut my ears!" That's my Mother!

One day I realized Mother was feeling uncomfortable living alone. She seemed uncertain and, maybe, a bit afraid?

When we asked if she would like to come live with one of us, she didn't hesitate in saying yes. I saw, at once, the relief in her eyes.

And so, it was, that that New Year's Eve we were all together at the Wheatley's.

It was Mother; Charlotte and Wheat; Glen and Gail; Maurice and Miriam; and Moi. We played games, ate and drank and toasted in 1992. Norman and Beverley, with their two girls, came by the next day. We were able to get pictures.

1992

Each year of my life has been filled with fun and exciting times, as in 1992.

It began with a trip to San Antonio where Laurie and I took a day trip to Gruene, Tx. It is a little town on the Guadalupe River. We had lunch in an old mill that had been converted into a restaurant. It was right on the river. As we ate our lunch, we watched the river, as it was in a flood stage and had flooded the road. We walked down to the river where two children were playing in the water. I snapped a picture and later painted a picture of them.

It was during that visit that the family took me to Paseo Del Rio Fiesta on the River

Walk. The River Walk!! Now that is something to experience. It is on the San Antonio River that runs through the downtown of San Antonio.

In 1938 the "San Antonio River Beautification Project," began the evolution of making this site into the present 2.5-mile-long River Walk. The River Walk is a city park and network of walkways along the banks of the San Antonio River, *one story* beneath the streets of San Antonio. Amazing! There are stores, a theater, a hotel, bridges that cross from side to side, beautiful planting, lots of things you can't imagine. One parks above on the street and takes a stairway to the park below. It really is quite an experience!

1992: Trip to Norway

In March I went to Norway! There is quite a story here and I must tell it from the beginning. So, lend an ear.

My friend from church, Evelyn Dettner, and her husband had hosted an exchange student, Thomas Stepanik from Norway. When he tried to commit suicide, his family came to take him home. Evie makes lasting friendships and when his mother Dana invited Evie to come for a visit, she was thrilled, but wanted someone to go with her. She had found inexpensive plane fare and lodgings would be free. Of course, I would go! I was so happy she thought of me to ask.

It was evening when we landed in Oslo where Thomas picked us up and drove us to his home in Kongsberg. (My first experience seeing a roundabout in a street.) His folks ran a Hostel so our room was small with 2 beds. There was a sort of lounge nearby where they brought us a snack of cheese and smoked salmon (ug).

(When I downsized and moved, I gave Evi my album so I haven't any pictures to remind me of the many things we did, but I do remember the significant things.)

We didn't meet the family until the next day, which included Dana and Mr. Stepanik, and 3 sons—Thomas, the oldest, Anthony, and Martin, who was about 12. He was learning English in school and wanted to talk to us so he could learn firsthand. He was cute and that was fun. Anthony would come into our room, sit on Evie's bunk and talk to me, (for Evie was often out with Thomas). Anthony talked about Norway, its immigration problems. He wasn't in favor of immigrants coming into his country. (Guess we aren't the only country having that problem, and that was years ago.)

Evie could speak German, and though it wasn't Norwegian she could converse enough to shop. So, we shopped. I bought a Norwegian sweater with silver clasps instead of buttons. They have a lot of silver but it is different from what we are used to. It has a burnished finish and doesn't tarnish. Dana gave me a small silver vase and a candle holder when we left for home. She gave Evie a beautiful cut glass bowl.

One day Thomas took us sightseeing. We drove through Oslo, then to

Holmenkollen, a ski jumping, recreation area in Oslo. It is known for its famous, eponymous, ski jumping hill, which has hosted ski jumping competitions since 1892.

Thomas drove us to the top where we could see the skier take off. It didn't seem to be a competition. We could see them jump into the air but not the landing. It was exciting, to be up there.

The best part of the trip was our ship ride on the North Sea to Trondheim.

Evie had a cousin and aunt living there and we would be staying with them. We traveled from Kongsberg by train. If the bridge hadn't been covered as we traveled along the edge of a mountain side, I would have been terrified. As I looked out through the side boards of the bridge, there was nothing! But I wasn't going to dwell on how far it might be to the bottom just enjoy the moment.

Bergen was our destination where we were to board the ship to Trondheim. It was rumored that it didn't snow in Bergen. Ha! There was at least 6 inches of slush.

Before going to the ship, we first had to visit the library, which, fortunately, was near the train station. Evi wanted to research her fatherinlaw's brother who was an Olympic gold medal winner for pole vaulting. She found a paper all about him and was shocked to find he was a Nazi sympathizer. She didn't like her fatherinlaw and was looking forward to telling him "his brother was a Natzie sympathizer."

That taken care of, we walked to the pier and boarded the ship. It was a ship that connected the small cities within the Fjords to civilization. It carried mail, supplies of all kinds, passengers, going to and from home, as well as people going north on holiday.

We were traveling by night and wouldn't get to Trondheim until early morning. We had a cabin with single double bunks and a tiny bathroom you walk in and back out. Evi was young and athletic back then, so she took the upper bunk. I remember that when we were in the open North Sea, I would slide to the foot of the bunk, then slide to the head, with the waves. When in the fjords all was calm and level.

Early on, while it was still light, we did go ashore at one of the little towns. We looked around but didn't buy anything. I wish I had

my album for pictures and reminders.

I don't remember much about the visit with her cousin. They were very welcoming. The next day was Sunday and we did go to an old Lutheran Church, which was interesting. But I best remember the dinner dessert of cloud berries and whipped cream! Cloud berries grow in the mountains and close to the ground and are difficult to pick. For that reason, I refrained from asking for seconds, though I wanted very much to do so. I still remember how tasty they were.

The trip back to Kongsberg was by train. There was little snow that year, but the countryside was scenic with small hillside villages and an occasional Stave Church. What is a Stave Church? I went to Google and found this: A stave church is a medieval wooden Christian church building once common in north western Europe. The name derives from the building's structure of post and lintel construction, a type of timber framing where the loadbearing orepine posts are called stave. Unique to Norway, they are medieval yet elegant symbols of Christianity's initial foothold into a country whose Viking era and ancient gods were a recent memory. Architecturally the stave churches are quite impressive. Made only of wood, some of them have survived for as many as 800 years. (I love "google"!)

Thomas was supposed to meet us at the train station when it got in. No Thomas anywhere, Evi decided we should walk back to the hostel. So, dragging our suitcases we started to walk, finally making it back to the Hostel. Then Thomas arrives and tells us he was there all the time and we just didn't see him. I guess the exercise was good for us.

Norway will always be a special country for me. I got to see it more intimately than if I were on a tour. I met the people and they were all so friendly. Dana and I still correspond through letters and Email.

COVID19 Insert • March 2020

As I sit here writing about my past, my mind can't stop dwelling on the present, TODAY! It is March 25, 2020. For over a week, now, we have been living under a terrible cloud. We are living with a great fear of a new illness called the Coronovirus.

It began in China. It swept through that country and is now spreading into every country throughout the world. The maps show most red dots in Korea, Italy and the US.

It is a respiratory disease and we have nothing, yet, to combat it. It is transmitted from person to person through contact with anything that has droplets, from a sneeze or cough, on it. Or being in front of someone sneezing or coughing.

All governments, in an attempt to curb this virus, have shut down all unessential businesses, closed all schools, restaurants, bars, theaters, etc. They have cautioned people to stay at home, work from home when possible.

Here at Sunrise Senior Living, my abode, all possible precautions have been taken. We are not to go outside the grounds—we may walk outside for the campus is lively. We are not to have visitors, unless it is a caregiver. Our meals are brought to our apartments, as is the mail or deliveries. Our temperatures are taken every morning. All employees are carefully screened each day. Activities have continued but we must sit 6 feet apart.

My family, my loved ones are all OK. They limit their shopping, but people are buying up large quantities so stores have empty shelves. Many people are buying online.

Joanne & Rick and Sandy are looking after my needs—I'm so blessed!!

Children and people over 60 are most vulnerable. I worry about Rick & Joanne and they worry about me.

Now that folks are homebound, they find time to catch up on procrastinated jobs. Rick told me he has cleaned the garage, the deck and today, it's raining, he will clean closets. Lisa called to say she bought, online, a fire pit. Yesterday she built a fire, for the first time in her life, and they had somemores.

Life goes on. We're at War with a disease and we will adapt to the hardships, and we will win.

Yesterday I posted on the bulletin some funny picture of wild animals doing funny things. We must keep our sense of humor!!

1992 • Family

When I couldn't find the photo album for 1993, '94, and '95, I was stymied.

Where is it? Where are all the pictures to help me remember those years? With these shutin days, because of the Coronovirus, I was cleaning out shelves and guess what? Down on the bottom shelf of the book case was a box of photos. I had never put those pictures into an album.

So, here we go again, back to 1992.

February 25th we celebrated Gerritt's 10th birthday. It was a memorable day, for we took a hike to Daniel's Mill Pond. There had been a

Mill there and a small community, but now only the remains of the old mill stand.

When Dick & Vi came for their spring visit, they were here in time to see the "Ships of Discovery," The Nina, Pinta, and Santa Maria. It was sponsored by Spain "92" Foundation and the City of Annapolis. The ships were anchored at the Annapolis City

Dock and were available to board and tour, for a price of $4.00 for seniors. We boarded but found the quarters very claustrophobic. Do

you remember why those ships are historically important? Of course, they were the ship that took Columbus on his first trip to the New World.

It was the need to introduce her new family to her extended family back east that brought Laurie back for a visit. It was July, and Alma & Ray, and Lillian & Dave made the trip down from Cleveland for the big occasion.

No, I didn't have rooms to sleep everyone, but Laurie, Greg and their children stayed with Lila, Greg's mother. (Didn't I have to share?!?) That was very convenient, for she lived only about a quarter mile away—one could walk it, if so inclined.

The gathering became even more festive when Charlotte & Wheat came with my Mother, and Rick and his family brought steamed crabs, (because Alma loved them so).

The weather was perfect. We were outside on the patio where it was cool and comfortable.

It was wonderful having Laurie and family here. That first week we visited the Naval Academy. Mark especially enjoyed the museum with the old nautical equipment and pictures of old naval vessels. We had lunch at the Amish Market just outside Annapolis. That was a new experience for them. The children didn't know about the Amish, nor had they ever seen an Amish horse and buggy.

Laurie and children extended their visit for another week. (They stayed with me, ha!) That week we celebrated my Birthday. (The Wheatleys were here for that, too.) We spent a day seeing the sights in Washington, DC. I am always awed when looking at Abe Lincoln and hoped the children felt that way too. We looked up at the Washington Monument but decided there were too many steps to climb.

Another day we joined Eileen, Daryl and Gerritt for a tour of Fort McHenry. The museum there exhibited the actual Flag that was flying when Francis Scot Key wrote the StarSpangled Banner. Imagine! The view atop the

gun parapets gave one's imagination a trip back in history. One could see the whole battle scene—the rockets red glare, bombs bursting in air.... I must ask Sandy if she remembers going there and seeing the cargo ships plying their way up and down the Chesapeake Bay?

The grand finale was a day spent at the Moran Cottage on Stony Creek. There they swam, canoed, and just played, with cousins, Daryl and Gerritt.

Mr. Moran gave everyone a boat ride out to the Chesapeake Bay where he showed off his new depth finder. Very impressive! He always had such gadgets that interested his grandsons.

As soon as Daryl & Gerritt were old enough they joined Boy Scouts, and Rick and Eileen became leaders. The whole family was deeply involved with camping, meetings and doing the tasks necessary to

pass the badges and rise up in the ranks. At the end of each year there was an awards picnic. I did enjoy attending those and watching the boys proudly receive their wellearned awards.

Then Christmas arrived, with all it's joy and excitement.

Oh Golly. I'm looking at my album and see my children showing off the Christmas presents I gave them. They are all holding up tshirts from Nova Scotia, with puffins and whales on them. Now, the big question is, when did I go to Nova Scotia with Maurice and Miriam?

Chapter 20 • Trip to Nova Scotia

"Some of the best things in life are the people we love,
the places we've travel together, and the memories
we've made along the way." — Unknown

Camping with M & M, August 11 to 30, 1992

The trip M & M and I took camping in Michigan was such fun, we decided we should take another trip and go to Nova Scotia. It was decided that they would leave Salisbury and drive directly to Annandale, NJ, where our younger brother, Norman, lived. I would meet them there. That was August 11, 1992. That was the beginning of a wonderful new adventure!

I left home at 10:15, drove Ritchie Hwy to 695, goofed and took the Essex exit, backtracked and finally was headed north on I95. The day was hot and humid. The sky, mostly sunny, but occasional dark clouds, threatened a storm. But I was happy! Happy to be behind the wheel of my trusty Red Sable. I felt free. Do you know that feeling?

The trip to Norman's was uneventful, tho there was some

construction. I did stop to take a Buffern for a neck ache and to call Bev for final directions. That dark cloud was now directly overhead and it began to rain. I had no trouble locating Norman's place and I arrived

around 2:45, before the real storm let loose, and before Maurice and Miriam arrived.

Bev gave me a tour of her home. It is a beautiful house—light, airy, situated in the middle of two acres of land. To the back there was a wooded area. The interior was lovely, just as one would expect, with Bev's charming good taste. Many of Mother's old pieces had been refinished and were strategically placed for design and comfort. A page out of House Beautiful.

Since I had arrived before anyone else, Bev and I had time to catch up on family gossip. I could tell she wasn't feeling well, and as we talked, she said she had Graves' Disease. She described her symptoms, and they seemed so much like Laurie's that I thought, "she must have Fibromyalgia, too." I was able to give her a treatment before we left, and she said it gave her some relief. Oh, for a magic wand!!

Norman arrived home from work around 5:00pm and Maurice and Miriam around 6:15. They were slower getting here, because of the road construction and the storm.

Did I mention that Bev is an extraordinary cook? Sort of on the gourmet side. She served us crab cakes, Maryland style, Ohio green

beans, New Jersey corn, their own homegrown tomatoes and broccoli salad. Wow it was good!

After such indulgence, we all needed a walk before enjoying dessert. Bev had baked a cake!

As we sat around the table, eating cake, we planned our route for the next day. We were headed to Maine, then north to Canada. After some discussion, Norman suggested a route we could take, and drew us a map. We were all set.

It was after 10pm when Kendra arrived home from her

work. We wanted to visit with her a bit, too. Of course, that meant another cup of coffee and another piece of cake. Oh, sooo good!!

The next morning, I looked out the window and saw the sun rising up over the hill, in the distance, and thought, "What a perfect day to travel!"

After breakfast of Bev's delicious homemade pumpkin muffins, and with Norman's written directions in hand, we were on the road.

We traveled the big highways, bypassing New York City, lunching and filling the gas tanks in Danville, through Connecticut, then north, touching New Hampshire and into Maine. Miriam did such a good job navigating, we rolled right along enjoying the scenery. We pulled into Wells State Park, near Sturbridge Mass. around 6:30.

When you don't use it, you lose it, and it was obvious I hadn't pitched my tent for some time. However, I finally had it all set up, just as Miriam called me to supper. I was ready for veggies stir fried! She is an amazing camp cook! She can make a feast out of leftovers.

We cleaned up, then went exploring. There was a lake, of sorts, and a beach for swimming. We walked down to the lake. It was a very steep path. And you know what? The path seemed even steeper as we walked back to camp. We were still puffing as we planned our route for tomorrow.

I guess I got it right, setting up camp last evening, for I had a good night's sleep and was raring to go the next morning. We were on the road by 9:30. I was excited to be going into Canada and camping at Fundy National Park. We had read about the fast, high tides of Fundy Bay, and I was intrigued, and wanted very much to see it!

The driving was easy with less traffic, but we had to backtrack twice when Maurice made a wrong turn. He was so upset, by this, he became almost ill. (This was a brother I didn't know). I felt so sorry, but couldn't remedy it.

The landscape through Maine was lush and green, with lots of evergreen trees and very pretty flowers along the road. It was a spiked lavender flower, that Maurice said was "loose strife". He is so knowledgeable about nature stuff.

We had lunch at a Rest Stop along the Maine Turnpike A chicken sandwich and a Dr Pepper, at the Burger King. We made frequent stops, for Maurice was still upset and feeling ill. Poor Guy!

Being an old hand at camping, Maurice had lists and maps of campsites along our route, so we knew where we would be camping each night. We located the Pleasant Lake Shores camp grounds, a private campground, just south of the Canadian border, and checked in. We had decided to wait until morning to make the border crossing into Canada.

The site was damp and mosquitoes were a big problem, Needless to say, I quickly set up my tent for sleeping, then retreated to the camper for supper and council. Later, Maurice built a fire, figuring the smoke would keep the mosquitoes away, while we roasted marshmallow. Maurice brought out his harmonica and we spent a lovely evening, roasting marshmallow and singing around the campfire. Maurice is really quite good with the harmonica, and Miriam has a lovely voice. I can keep a tune if someone leads.

Notice the stone wall in the picture. We, Maurice especially, figured they must be very old, probably a border for a pasture. The builder must have been very skilled, to construct a wall that had endured the elements for so many years. Beautiful in a rough way.

My journal tells me I decided to sleep on the ground that night. I wonder why? Too lazy to set up the camp cot? Probably.

I did sleep well, after crawling out of the sleeping bag and lying on top of it, covering myself with the blanket and my coat. I kept hearing a constant plunk, plunk that made me curious. What was making that sound? When I stepped out of my tent early in the morning, I looked up into the thick branches of hickory trees, and realized the tree had been dropping nuts during the night. Plunk, plunk. Curiosity satisfied.

It was a cold morning and the shower house was cold, but the water was blessedly hot, and felt wonderful! After a breakfast of cereal and English Muffin we were on the road to Bangor where we stopped for groceries and filled our gas tanks. Gas was cheaper in the US.

Crossing into New Brunswick, Canada was so exciting! I felt like a kid riding her first merrygoround. I'm having an adventure! I'm in another country! Imagine that!

The road to Calais was not a good road, often very bumpy. We stopped at a roadside eatery and had lunch. Miriam and I splurged and had my favorite—coconut cream pie. That made up for the bumpy road.

Calais is the official Border Crossing into Canada. Before driving across the border, we found a store and a bank, where I bought a battery lamp and battery and changed $300 US traveler's check into Canadian dollars.

Finally, we were in line to actually cross the border. M & M

went through without a glitch, but I was behind a slow vehicle and the attendant was chatting. I finally caught up with them at the pretty little Lighthouse Info Station. We collected the necessary information to Fundy National Park. I took some pictures and we were on our way.

Fundy National Park was really the starting point of this new adventure, "Camping through Nova Scotia." That was where our

adventure really began. Each evening we would sit in the camper and discuss where and what we would do the next day. Maurice had guidebooks and maps. He was full of ideas of places and things we should see. He was a wonderful tour guide. He and Miriam were seasoned campers and I was a novice, ready and willing to follow their lead.

So here we were at Fundy National Park, along the shores of Fundy Bay, noted for its high and fast tides. I was so looking forward to watching this amazing feat of nature.

We entered the park and bought $30 passes, for we intended to stay two nights. We soon discovered this park covered many acres, for we had to travel 18 more miles to our designated campsite, Point Wolfe. It was dark by then and I needed a flashlight to pitch my tent and set up for the night.

It turned cold during the night and the morning proved to be breezy. We needed to dress warmly, for we were planning to do some hiking. It was sweatsuits and coats, and a hot breakfast kind of weather. Scrambled egg beater with tomatoes and sausage was just the thing!

Taking the Sable, we began our sightseeing day. First stop was Point Wolfe. We took the path that led down to the Wolfe River. The river was narrow but the beach was wide, sandy with small rocks, almost pebbles. I picked up some pretty ones.

From where we stood, we could see what looked like the delta, where the river flowed into the Bay of Fundy.

Turning in the other direction, we could see the covered bridge we had crossed last night, when we entered the park. The bridge crossed over a dam, used for flood control. At one side of that construction was a ladder to enable spawning fish to get over the dam and up into the river.

It was low tide, and where we stood, we could see how far the high tide had reached.

We drove up to the bridge, then stood at the side of the road, looking down to the Bay. The tide was coming in, so I took 2 pictures 15 minutes apart, of the incoming tide. Notice the water marks in the sand.

Maurice especially liked waterfalls, so he was looking forward to seeing the famous Dickson Falls. We drove to the parking area and took the trail leading to Dickson Falls. It was a boardwalk with a railing, and steps, lots of steps going down, through a rough wooded area. We were following a creek. There was a high bank on the other side. I'm not sure how far down we were, when we saw that the opposite bank was covered with butterflies. All sizes and colors, flying hither and thither. Most amazing sight! Sort of spooky too.

As we continued walking down the trail steps, we could look back and see Dickson Falls, and the creek, as it cascaded down the rocky terrain.

It was lunchtime and after all that exercise, for we had to climb back up those stairs, we were starved!

Alma was the little fishing town we had driven through on our way to the park.

It was nestled in a cove off the Bay of Fundy, where The Tides of Fundy played such a significant part in the lives of the residents. When the tide is high, the men sail their boats out to do their fishing. When the tide is out, the boats left behind, sit in a cradle in the mud. Fascinating, don't you think?

We had a big lunch of hot turkey sandwiches with potatoes, carrots, peas and coleslaw, hoping for enough left over to take back to camp for another meal. Miriam could take those leftovers and make a feast! Always amazed me!

Deciding we wanted to explore a bit more of this interesting little town, we walked up the street, found a general store, where I bought postcards to send to grandchildren, and where we all enjoyed a soft ice cream cone, as we watched a fishing boat come into port. Tide was up.

Everywhere you looked there were flowers in bloom. They were so pretty! We headed back to the park, but stopped at the main building to take pictures of the beautiful flower gardens there.

Next, on our agenda, was to walk the trail to Devil's Half Acres. It was an awesome trail, spanning three chasms. There were views of natural disruptions of the earth, that formed these chasms and downed huge trees.

We were still marveling at all we had seen, as we drove back to camp.

Supper was over and it was still light. Such a lovely evening should not be wasted. It was our last night in Fundy Park, so why not walk out to Point Wolf again and check the tide. It was amazing! The tide was out, revealing a large expanse of sand, all the way out to the Bay of Fundy.

It was the Sabbath, so after breakfast, we had a Bible reading and some prayer time. We would often say grace at supper time, too. It's impossible to overlook God when we see his marvelous creations as we travel.

The morning was chilly and raining. We broke camp and headed north.

As we passed through the village of Alma the tide was out. There was a mud flat reaching out about a quarter of a mile. I noticed the large V-shaped cradles along the banks, where the boats would sit, keeping them out of the mud. Ingenious, I thought.

We were on our way to Monkton and the ferry that would carry us to Prince Edward Island. But first, there was a must stop at the Rocks. We parked high on a cliff and walked down, I know it was at least 100, steps, to the beach. On the beach were massive rock for-

mations called "flower pots". There were caves too. The tide was low so we were able to walk among those monoliths. However, it was maybe 15 minutes later, a loud speaker warned us that the tide was coming in and we should start coming back up, or we would be trapped. Maurice had his video camera on the ready and taped the water as it covered some small rocks on the beach. It was fascinating to watch! Within 30 seconds the rocks were covered.

Before we reached Moncton, we stopped at a gazebo along the Petitcodiac River.

Maurice had timed it just right, for we were just in time to watch the river try to flow into the Fundy Bay, but the tides push it back on itself, creating a tidal bore. We watched this 10inch wave. It looked like a log rolling back up the river. It was fast and covered about a quarter mile in 10 minutes. This phenomenon happens twice a day and we were there in time to watch it. What a rare experience for us! (My tour guide had checked on the tide time so we would arrive in time to watch this Tidal Bore. I told you he was good!)

We had lunch near Monkton, before boarding the ferry, then took advantage of the 45 minute crossing to sit in the lounge and study the map of Prince Edward Island, our destination for that day.

We arrived at Prince Edward Island National Park in time for supper. Our site was on a high cliff, overlooking the beach of the Gulf of St. Lawrence. The beach was rocky with flat red rocks, except where they had cleared for swimming. We were near the bathroom, too, which always made me happy! There was a potty in M & M's camper so they weren't as concerned about the location of the bathrooms as I was.

After searching around, we found a flat spot to set up my tent. We cooked and ate dinner in the shelter that had an oldfashioned wood stove, and a picnic table. The park does not allow campfires. Supper was hot dogs and baked beans, zucchini and carrot cake. Delicious!

These summer days gave us light long after supper, so we took my car and drove around, orienting ourselves. It started to rain, and guess what? When we returned to camp, we found my tent sitting in a puddle of water. That explained why there were no flat places! With Maurice's help I soon had it sitting high and dry. I was glad I had on my Hush Puppy Shoes. They are almost waterproof.

It continued raining all night, but I was high and dry and slept well. I did find puddles in the two front corners of the tent, when I got up. Nothing to worry about.

After a leisurely breakfast, M & M drove the camper to a special place to dump the waste, (necessary with an inhouse potty). Then we headed out to explore the Island.

When on Prince Edward Island one must visit the home of Anne of Green Gables.

There was a replica of the house where she grew up with her grandparents, who tended the post office, which is part of the house. The house is now a museum, but the post office is still functioning as a Canadian Post Office.

We browsed the museum, just the usual stuff of that era, then I bought stamps and mailed Sandy's package and the postcards. How convenient was that?

It was lunch time and we were hungry. After some driving around looking for a place to eat, we ended up buying picnic food and eating at a little park we had passed. There were no fast food places in the country but as we neared the city there were many. Oh well, picnicking was more fun anyway. We did stop at a

McDonald's for a cup of coffee, an apple bran muffin and a yogurt ice cream cone. We liked to eat healthy!!?

We continued on to Charlottetown, the capital of Prince Edward Island, and into Victoria Park. It is a lovely big park, bordering the harbor that leads out to the Northumberland Strait. An ideal location for defending the Island.

There was a parking area near the entrance. We left the car and walked through part of the park.

The lighthouse was pictur-esque as was the view down the harbor toward the Strait.

There were a dozen or so old cannons set up, pointing out

to the harbor ready to defend the island. I wondered, "against whom?" Now, as I research the history, there was a lot of conflict back in the 1700s and 1800s with England, France, and New

England. The final outcome was a new Province for Canada, Prince Edward Island.

Before leaving the park, we made a stop at the visitor's center, where there were lots of displays and gifts. We picked up several maps, hoping they would give us more information than the ones we had. There were lots more of the Island to see.

It rained all night, but no puddles in my tent this morning. Showered, washed my hair, and joined M & M for breakfast around 8:30. It was drizzling or sprinkling off and on.

There was no set plan for the day, we would just drive around the countryside and stop if something looked interesting.

Prince Edward Island is long and narrow, situated within the Gulf of St. Lawrence. Lots of beaches. We stopped at the Cavendish Boardwalk for a look around. It was much like Ocean City with the sandy beach on one side and shops and eateries on the other.

We ate lunch at a McDonald's. There was something we don't see at Ocean City, and that was a lobster sandwich. M & M enjoyed theirs. I had a McChicken sandwich but it had too much mayonnaise on it. I could only eat half. Should have tried the lobster.

The rain was so persistent, we decided to find a KMart and buy umbrellas. I bought a red one. Is that surprising?

Galway on the Sea was our next stop. It is a very famous resort hotel. That piqued our curiosity. What did a "famous" hotel look like? We went inside. It was polished, rustic and GRAND! It was once the summer home for wealthy Alexander McDonald, who was president of Standard Oil. He had named it after his home in Scotland. Now, it is owned by the National Bank but another party runs it.

As we were leaving, Miriam attempted to get into the wrong red car. She just couldn't understand why the door wouldn't open. We laughed and kidded her a lot about that.

It was raining but we still wanted to see some lighthouses. That shouldn't be a problem with so much coastline. Yes, there were lighthouses, but the day was overcast and not bright enough to photograph them. So be it!

We had supper and planned for tomorrow.

I should explain about how we found campsites. As I said, M&M were seasoned campers. They belonged to several "Membership" Camping groups, one of which was Coast to Coast. There was an annual membership fee which allowed them to camp free or at a discount at these camps. Some of these camps might have a clubhouse with restaurant; there might be a swimming pool and playground for children. Others offered fewer amenities, just campsites with bath houses, and maybe an electric hookup.

*Maurice had our trip all mapped out as to where we could stay. It could be at one of these camps or it could be at a State or National Park. Some of those had extra amenities, too. There was always one absolute requirement! The bathrooms **had to be near our campsite!***

The sun was shining! It was a beautiful day! We were ready for it! My tent was soaked and I had to pack it in a plastic bag. No time to lay it out to dry, for we were moving on.

Everything was damp, or wet and soggy on the outside. The wool blanket smelled up my car. Such is life tent camping! But I was having a good time!

As we were leaving Prince Edward Island, I knew I would always have fond memories of this Island, of its gently rolling hills, and peaceful, pastoral countryside. I will remember how clean everything seemed, and peaceful.

When we boarded the ferry going to Prince Edward Island, we did not pay a fee. That seemed strange. But, not so strange when one thinks about it. Once on the island, there was no other way to get back to the mainland, but by ferry. It was on the trip back to the mainland that one paid a fee.

We boarded the Woods Island Ferry, paying $7.90 a person and $25.75 per car. M & M were saved $2.00 for being seniors. I looked too young. Can you believe that?

This was a smaller ferry than the one we came over on, but it had a dining room/snack bar. We were able to settle down, for the next hour and a half, and make plans and write cards. We wanted to drive the Cabot Trail, on Cape Brenton Is.

We filled out gas tanks on the mainland before crossing to Cape Breton Is. Then discovered gas was cheaper on the island. Wouldn't you know?

We found the Coast to Coast Campground Maurice had chosen, Silver Springs Campground. I was a very unhappy camper, when

I realized the bathrooms were a quarter mile away. It seems this was a new campground. They were just getting started and had not yet set up all those comfortable amenities Coast to Coast is known for. It was too late to look for another campground, so I bit the bullet and set up my tent.

Then, we went shopping for ice and groceries.

Dinner was at the Barn, in the nearby town, where we received a 10% C to C discount. Well, at least that was something. There was a gift shop and a telephone, so we called Charlotte to see about Mother.

The evening ended on a very pleasant note, for it had stopped raining and the evening was warm and dry. Maurice built a fire. We toasted marshmallows, ate smores and talked. I was a bit worried about getting to the bathroom during the night.

I did get through the night without needing to go that ¼ mile to the bathrooms.

There was a heavy dew during the night, and the tent floor was wet. I put plastic bags down to keep my feet dry, then washed up and put my eyes in. (Did I mention I was wearing contact lenses? At night, I would take them out in the camper but put them on in the bathrooms.) After taking down the tent, I draped it over the table to dry the floor, while we ate breakfast.

Then it was off to Alexander Graham Bell's Museum. His home is nearby, where his family still resides.

The museum was beautifully landscaped, and looked out over a channel of water that flowed into Brae D'ord Lake. There were several channels visible, forming an interesting pattern of land and water. There were 2 red Adirondack chairs, beckoning someone to sit and enjoy the view.

I was excited to be traveling the Cabot Trail. I don't know what it was that intrigued me. I must have read something that had me romanticizing about it. I soon discovered it was all I had imagined.

The Cabot Trail circles Cape Breton Island. On the west, it climbs the mountain, following the coast of the Gulf St Laurence. When it reaches South Point it begins to descend along the coast of the Atlantic Ocean.

We began the Trail on the west side, at Chitticamp. Doesn't that word tickle your tongue? I love saying it!

We arrived at Cape Breton Highland National Park around 3pm, found a nice site, with a fireplace, for which we had to pay extra, and near the bathrooms. After settling in, we drove to the visitor's center. There were a lot of exhibits but my eyes were tired and I'm afraid I didn't appreciate them as much as I should.

The gift shop is always a magnet to me. I bought two cookbooks, one for Norm and Bev, and a blueberry one for Marge. She has prolific blueberry bushes.

There was a trail leading off our campsite, the Prarie Trail. We followed it to the Chiticamp River. It was lovely, as it gently cascaded over a rocky terrain. There was a rocky area, covered with wildflowers, rising up in the center of the river, dividing it. Very picturesque!

A quarter mile later we were back at camp and hungry. It was hot dogs over the open fire and leftovers. When we eat Miiam's leftovers we're sure to have a banquet! She's a wonder worker!!

We topped off the day by roasting marshmallows.

I was up early, but still, the bathroom was busy. There were only two stalls and one shower. It seemed I wasn't the only camper who wanted to get an early start on the day.

I pulled stakes and put the tent out to dry while we had breakfast, then we headed out to explore the little town of Cheticamp. I not only liked the name, I was delighted by the fact that it was an Acadian French town, and the residents all spoke French and English. They are ancestors of the Acadian French, in New Orleans. When I went on Google, I learned Nova Scotia, in the 1700's was once Acadia. Very interesting!

The town is on the shores of The Gulf of St. Lawrence. It has a population of 4000, extends along the coast for 4+ miles, and has stores, a scenic old church, and a residential area that is not on the coast but more inland.

Cheticamp Coop is a very successful consumer cooperative in the village. It offers a wide range of food, general merchandise and building supplies. It serves over 2,300 memberowners in the region and is governed by a ninemember Board of Directors (says Google).

We were curious about the island across the harbor so drove across the causeway to explore it. We followed the paved road to its end where a lobster fisherman had his home with a pier, boat, and lobster traps. It was very picturesque.

  We asked him about the lighthouse and he directed us back to a dirt road. that followed the inland shoreline, through the pastures and among the cows and one bull. This was all part of the Coop.

As we drove back, we could see across the harbor to the town of Cheticamp, and St Peters Church. With the mountain in the background, it was a photographer's delight! Well, of course, we stopped and took pictures. It was overcast so they probably wouldn't show the scene as it really is.

St Peters church is a Methodist church. M & M are good  Methodists and they wanted to go in. It is a very old church. The lovely building was erected in 1893, but the parish itself dates back to 1785.

We walked through the town, bought some fresh warm bread and headed back to camp, anxious for lunch and that fresh warm bread, with tomato, cheese and apple cream coffee cake. We were certainly eating well!

It was time to move on up the Cabot Trail. Beautiful picturesque scenery of winding mountain roads, tiny fishing villages and spectacular overlooks. We stopped for pictures but it was really too overcast for good pictures.

There was a Bog Trail leading off one overlook that Maurice wanted to walk. Miriam and I stayed dry in the camper.

We had traveled 23 miles, when we came to a little fishing village, Pleasant Bay.

We really didn't know what lay ahead and figured we had better fill the gas tanks before settling for the night.

I really don't recall how we came upon this particular campsite, but I do vividly recall that I refused to stay there. It meant pitching my tent in wet soggy ground. We had passed a motel, The Mountain View Motel, a few miles down the road. I said, "I'm going to spend the night at that motel, we just passed." They were going to stay put.

I drove to the motel and reserved one room for the night.

It was still early and we wanted to visit the tiny town of Red River. There was an interesting story of a fire, in 1941, that roared down the mountain and destroyed both Red River and Pleasant Bay. The towns were of sturdy stock and had recovered, for we saw no evidence of the disaster.

Golly, what incredible scenery!! It was rainy and dark clouds hovered over the landscape, not the best weather for picture taking. We decided to come back tomorrow, hoping the sun would peak through those dark clouds long enough for a couple of good photographs.

Dinner was at the motel. While we were eating Miriam announced that she was going to join me in the motel for the night.

Have I mentioned that Maurice is a bit tight with his money? He was not going to pay for lodging when he had a perfectly good camper in which to sleep.

The dinner was good, with Haddock for Maurice and Turkey roast with all the fixings for Miriam and Me. We topped it off with blueberry cobbler and ice cream.

After we finished eating, Maurice said, "I might as well join you and sleep in the motel, too." We laughed and kidded him a lot, later.

The motel manager was a friendly Scotsman who, when informed M & M would be staying too, let us have the room for no added cost. Maurice was happy!

It rained some during the night and we were all happy to have

spent the night in the motel. The next morning looked like it might clear up. After scrambled eggs and toast, slathered with butter (margarine isn't used here) we headed back to Red River. The sun was coming up. Perfect for picture taking! We were glad we returned.

We crested a hill and drove down into the town of Pleasant Bay. I remember seeing the quaint little houses painted red and blue and thinking how neat!

There was a long red building used for storing lobster cages;

and another red building was the fire station. All very tidy and convenient.

We continued climbing the Cabot Trail, until we came to the Macintosh Brook Trail, and decided to walk the short trail.

We crossed several bridges until we found the waterfalls. What is it about a waterfalls that is so enticing? Is it the sound of the water rushing over the high rocks, or seeing the water cascading down into the crevasse below? Perhaps it is both, that fill us with excitement and wonder.

I find I'm intrigued by so many things that are new to me. For instance, Lone Shieling. We walked the ½ mile trail to where the park had reproduced an authentic Scotland Shieling, a hut, or collection of huts, once common in wild or lonely places in the hills and mountains of Scotland and northern England.

We found a small round, stone building with thatched roof, perhaps 20ft. in diameter, with 2 square openings for windows. The stones were carefully layered, one on the other, no mortar. Amazing!

When the Scot shepherds migrated to Cape Breton Island in early 1700, they built such a croft, that housed both the shepherd and the sheep, depending on the weather. It was very primitive. I noted large flat stones creating benches around the inside wall. At least they didn't sit or sleep on the floor. Interesting, too, was the forest around it;  a large grove of Maple trees, some said to be 350 years old. The grove is said to be the largest stand of hardwood forest in the Maritimes.

We left the croft and followed the trail to the Grand Anise River. There the river fell over a rocky ledge forming another lovely waterfall cascaded down through the forest.

When it reached level ground it spread out, leaving small stones to be gathered by us.

There were only a few more miles to go, before rounding the tip of Cape Breton Island. It was quite a surprise to find the eastern side of the Island very different from what we had been seeing on the west side.

On the western side, the Cabot Trail had been an easy trip. We had gradually climbed, as we passed through small fishing villages, stopped at overlooks and hiked a side trail that beckoned.

Now, as we headed down the eastern side, we had to slip into low gear. We were suddenly on a steep winding mountain road. I gasped! How do I do this? I was a bit frightened, worried, very concerned, for I had no experience driving down steep curvy roads. My trusty Sable had automatic transmission; would I know how to go into low gear without stripping the gears. I told myself, "you have no choice, just do what feels right." So, I did. *(Later, after I had been home a few months, I did have to put in a new transmission.)*

Once I had overcome my anxiety, I realized we were looking out at the Atlantic Ocean. We followed the coast and stopped at an overlook to photograph the Aspy Fault.

We stopped at an inlet when we saw picnic tables and a toilet. The toilet was a pit toilet that had no inside door latch (that's camping for you).

After our picnic lunch, we drove on to another tiny inlet, Green Cove, where we walked out onto a rocky outcropping. The rock was

not like any other rocks I had ever seen. They were rather flat, as if pressed, with long white lines across many of them. Strange! There were signs, explaining that they were part of the Aspy Fault, and the result of the constant

movement and pressure within the fault. They are Samgamonian stones. The markings are called Dykes.

Later, I learned another interesting fact about this mountain. It is a continuation of the Appalachian Mountain Range. How about that?

The brochures we had collected suggested we be on the lookout for the island shaped like a whale. Sure enough, there it was, just as they said; a humongous whale, calmly lying out in the ocean. Oh, the wonders of nature!

One of the joys of traveling with M & M was their knowledge of the trees and flowers. When they saw something special, they would call me on my CB and point it out to me, such as the lovely groves of white birch trees, along the road to Ingonish

At Ingonish, we stopped at the Keltie Lodge. We decided it was too ostentatious for us. Give us a rustic campsite, any time. It was very impressive, tho, offering such luxuries as a swimming pool, golf course, white napkin dining, and a beautiful panoramic view.

This was the last stop on the Cabot Trail. We did it! We drove the Cabot Trail!

The quickest way to get back to Badeck was to take the Englishtown Ferry across the mouth of St Ann's Bay. It was a quaint little ferry pulled across the water by an electric cable. I seem to recall it could take only one car at a time. I went first and had to wait for M&M on the other side. As I drove off the boat, I noticed a stand along the side of the road, selling homemade fudge. When M & M drove off the ferry, we drove a few yards on to a little store, nearby, and bought ice cream cones. I told them about the fudge stand. My mouth watered. The fudge was tempting. Why not? Why not walk back and buy some fudge for later? It was such a lovely warm, sunny day. Why not? We were thoroughly enjoying ourselves! The fudge was very good, too!

We were soon back at Badeck and the Silver Springs campgrounds, but this night, we were near the bath house. Hallelujah!

There was a laundromat nearby, with a little eatery over it. While our clothes were washing

and drying, we ate dinner. It was a cabbage/veggie soup with a roll. Maurice's stomach had been unhappy, so he settled for coffee and a biscuit. $13.50, plus $1.00 for ice for the coolers.

I find it interesting, as I read my journal, that I listed all the costs of the laundry. I'm my brother's sister!??!

Laundry expenses: large load $1.50, small load $1.25, plus .25 for 4minute drying. We combined and used 1 large, 2 small and 3 drying times.

Back at camp I had to rearrange my bed for it was on a slope. I needed my head at the high end.

It had been a good night! no trip to the john! The dew was heavy, when I awoke at 7:00 and everything was wet, but wouldn't take long to dry.

It was the Sabbath, so after breakfast, we had our Bible study and prayers for a continued safe and enjoyable journey. By then everything was dry so we pulled up stakes and headed to Hallifax.

We stopped for gas at Whycocomaguh. Definitely a Scotish village, for the man at the gas station, who, by the way, as very nice, spoke with a scotish brogue when we introduced himself as Mr. MacCaulay. One meets the nicest people when traveling.

We drove across the Canso Causeway that connects Cape Breton Island to the Nova Scotia Peninsula. It is a rock filled road that carries two lanes of traffic, as well as a single track railroad. It is 2.84 miles long. I was interested and looked it up on Google.

Lunch stop was at Antigonish, where we tried to buy batteries for my camera and Maurice's watch. It was Sunday and every place was closed.

It had been steady, easy driving, causing Maurice to get sleepy. We pulled over so Miriam could take the wheel. She is a good driver and we sailed right along. As we neared Hallifax we looked for a Visitor's Center and saw one, but had trouble getting to it. We made several "u" turns that confused me and I lost them. I almost panicked, but with the CB we finally connected, found the info station and were given directions to a campground in Dartmouth. The twin city to Halifax.

The area is known for its lakes. Our campsite was at Lake Charles and near the beach.

It was lovely. We had to park the vehicles outside the campgrounds but it wasn't far to walk to our campsite. We settled in. I was becoming aware of a scratchy throat and a cough. Must be getting a cold, drat! So while M & M took a walk, I took a nap.

Supper was one of Miriam's delicious miracles, pasta with leftover turkey, Tang and vitamin C.

We planned the next day's trip into Halifax. Then called Charlotte. Mother was not doing well. She could no longer help

herself. She needed feeding, and lifting, and had an infection in her eyes. We would call again tomorrow.

Bed Time! I'll wear my sweats to bed. Maybe I can sweat this cold out of me.

I awoke at 7 to find a sunny day with a cold wind. Feeling some better. Still coughing, and my nose was running. At first, the nearby highway noise was distracting, and the wind off the lake

caused the tent to flap, but once asleep, I slept well.

Showered, then organized my things. Five rolls of film needed to be put somewhere. I would buy batteries this morning.

Miriam made sure I had hot Tang for breakfast and an English Muffin.

We left around 9:30, and headed to Halifax. After paying a $.75 toll, we crossed the MacEwen Bridge, into Halifax, and parked in a parking garage by the Harbor. We walked along the waterfront, where the Nova Scotia Tall Ship, the "Bluenose," was anchored. It was one of the Tall Ships that sailed into Baltimore during our 300 year celebration in 1976.

Among the sights in Halifax, our brochures recommended we see the Parade. I parked the car and we walked up George St to what is called The Grande Parade. It is a walled in area with the City Hall at one end and St Paul Angelican Church at the other.

Straight ahead of us, was the famous Clock Tower. *(From google: The clock tower is a three-tiered (three storey), irregular octagon tower built atop a one storey white clapboard building. The clock face is 4sided displaying Roman numerals. As with most clocks the "4" is shown as IIII for*  *aesthetic symmetry and not as IV. The clock mechanism is driven by three weights, gears, and a 13foot pendulum with the mechanism being housed in a cast iron frame located in the "clock room", immediately below the belfry. Its bell strikes hourly and quarterly and the durability of the mechanism [which dates to the original installation] is attributed to its*

slow movement. The Town Clock began keeping time for the garrison on October 20, 1803.) We took pictures.

As we were returning to the car, we passed a store selling Nova Scotia souvenirs. Just what I was looking for! I bought sweatshirts for the grandchildren. The shirts had Nova Scotia puffins on one and a whales on the other. It's always fun buying for the grandchildren.

We drove to the Citadel, situated on a hill overlooking Halifax Harbor. Well placed to defend Halifax.

A very nice and well informed college student guided us on a tour of the fort. We were seeing it as it was in 1800. Everyone was dressed in period attire. The parading soldiers were wearing kilts and carrying guns and drums, the women were in dark, long dresses and aprons. She told us this was the fourth fort constructed on this site.

On hearing what sounded like a bagpipe, we walked in that

direction. Sure enough, it was a Scotishattired man, playing the bagpipes. He was standing near a tiny hut where a woman was sitting listening. We enjoyed listening, too.

Looking over the wall, out at the harbor, we could see Halifax city and boats in the harbor. It was another panoramic view to photograph.

The next recommended attraction was The Public Gardens. There were actually many gardens, within one garden. There was such a variety of flowering plants, I couldn't begin to name them all. There were two ponds with ducks and swans, beautiful old trees, that M & M recognized and admired, a fountain and guess what, an ice cream shop.

I snapped a picture of two, happy children sitting on the ground feeding the pigeons. Watching them made us happy, too.

Getting out of Halifax was no problem, but after crossing the MacDomald bridge and on the Dartmout side of the lake, we got all fouled up. I should have checked the map before we started out. When we finally found familiar territory we stopped to buy groceries.

We were disgruntled and tired, so supper was an easy one of hot dogs, eaten out on a picnic table. Not much to cleanup.

Before turning in, we called Norman to tell him we wouldn't be back as scheduled, for we were extending our trip another week. He said they were taking Kendra back to school in Michigan that week. We needn't stop by, for they wouldn't be there.

We were early risers, getting up around 6:30 or 7:00 each morning. This morning I found the tent wet from a heavy dew. It had dried by the time we finished breakfast.

Last night, as we planned our itinerary for today, we decided not to go see Peggy's Cove, although it was one of the recommended attractions. It couldn't be as wholesome and picturesque as the little fishing villages on Cape Breton Island. Peggy's Cove would be more touristy. Not to our liking. So, we headed west toward home.

We would take another week to stop and see the sights along the way.

The Shubenacadia Canal links Halifax with the Bay of Fundy. We walked along one of the many trails that branch off the canal.

There were bridges to cross. Waterlilies were floating, ducks swimming, loones crying their plaintive call. M & M identified a kingfisher's call. It was lovely!

As we continued on our way, we made many stops, mostly pit stops (we're old). Near Amhert, we stopped at the post office and a small mall. I mailed my cards. At the mall, I bought a sweatsuit, you know, shirt and pants to match, for $36.95. I had wanted a set like this one for some time.

We had crossed into New Brunswick, Canada and were on our way to Waterborough and the Mohawk Camping Grounds, our destination. I insisted on a campsite near the bath house. It also had an electric hookup that cost an extra $16.59. Maurice didn't fuss. Bless his heart!

The campground was on Grand Lake, a large lake but it was misty and overcast, so we couldn't see it clearly or very far into it.

We cooked hot dogs and ate out on the picnic table. No Mosquitos! We planned for tomorrow hoping to camp at Etna, as we did coming. It was still early but we were tired and the night was cold so we turned in.

My journal says I had spread my sleeping bag on the ground. (It wasn't the first time, from what I've been reading. Was I too lazy to put up the cot? Or too tired?) Whatever, the ground was hard and sloping, but apparently, I slept well.

I awoke to find a fine mist in the air. A lady in the bathhouse said she heard rain was predicted.

I quickly pulled stake before my tent got wet. Then, knowing we would be crossing the border back into the US, I organized my receipts and purchases, for we would get some refund on the tax we had paid on out purchases.

It was a good, sort of casual day. We often stopped for one thing or another. Pit stops, KMart for a battery for Maurice's watch.

Nearing the border, there was the stop to retrieve our tax money, $25. A bit farther on, in Houlton, we exchange our Canadian money back to US dollars. We had gained 15 cents going in and lost 12 coming out.

We passed a couple of roadside stands, and stopped to buy green beans, onions, and green peppers. At another, we bought fresh corn.

We arrived at Two Rivers campground in time for super. We were really looking forward to a supper of all those fresh veggies.

Our campsite was along a river that joined another river, perhaps 100 yard down from our campsite. I tried to get pictures but it was really too hazy.

It was a warm summer evening and we ate those delicious fresh veggies out on the picnic table. Later, we called Charlotte; Mother failing, Charlotte lost Mother's teeth.

I needed to get home!

I called Laurie, too. She said she had just gotten my cards  and had been worried about us. I wrote the cards but couldn't always find a post office to mail them.

Another misty morning. The tent was wet, but only on the outside. It had dried by the time we finished breakfast. While we were eating breakfast we were entertained, watching a small boy, sitting down by the water, feeding the ducks. The ducks were climbing all over each other as they tried to be first for the handout. The river was pretty, in spite of the weather.

We were soon on the road again, following the Kennobee River. As we drove into New Hampshire I noted so many of the farms had their building all connected. That made sense. The winters were severe, cold with heavy snow. Having the buildings connected saved the

226

farmer the difficulty of plowing through drifts of snow, or buffeting snow storms, getting to the animals.

The farms were usually very neat, the buildings white with brown trim. I indicated to M & M that I wanted to stop and get a picture. There was a man out washing his porch as I snapped the picture.

We followed the Androscoggin River for a while, making several pit stops on the way, and stopping in Gorham for gas

Then we began climbing the mountains.

Maurice explained that the road followed the passes, or notches made as the many mountains formed. They seemed to be undulating and we never climbed very high.

Having heard so much about the "Old Man of the Mountain," we didn't want to miss seeing it. There were signs along the road giving direction to the parking area where one could walk to the best viewing site. We parked our vehicles, then walked down to the path to a small lake. It was very picturesque. The water was so clear and clean. Several children were wading.

We stood and looked up and off to the right. What we saw was awesome! A perfect profile of a man's head protruding from the stony outcropping on the side of the mountain. The "Old Man of the Mountain"!

I don't remember when, but shortly after our visit we heard he had broken away from the mountain. How fortunate we were to have seen it before its demise.

The day had turned cloudy as if to rain. We found the Hancock campsite in the White Mountain National Forest campgrounds, and quickly set up camp. I was getting very proficient in setting up my tent and settling in. I was ready, let it rain!

We spent the evening in the camper, reading maps and planning the route for tomorrow. The Kancamagus Highway is reportedly a very scenic highway. Traveling a scenic highway was our preference. It would take us through the White Mountains.

It rained a lot during the night. My camp cot extended across the tent, touching it at both ends. Where it touched the tent, water seeped in, so my cot was damp at both ends.

I chose to sleep nearer the foot. The

outside of the sleeping bag was wet, but inside I was toasty warm and dry. The tent being nylon would dry quickly.

Up at 6:00 for a trip to the outhouse. No bathhouse, just a pit toilet. No running water or tooth brushing, I went into the camper to put my eyes in.

We had planned a busy day, so were soon on the road. We followed the map, found the Kancamagus Highway, and enjoyed the mountain scenery as we turned north to Conway Glen. Lunch was at a little restaurant in the small town of Bartlett. BarBQue chicken, corn on the cob, and biscuits for only $3.50. It was very good and enough to doggie bag for dinner.

We continue on to Breton Woods, on the slopes of Mt.

Washington. This is where the famous 1944 Monetary Conference was held. "It was the gathering of representatives of 44 countries, to establish The World Bank, set the Gold Standard at $35 an ounce,  and chose the American dollar as the backbone of international exchange. The meeting provided the world with a badly needed post war currency stability." (says Google.)

Next stop was the famous Cog Railroad, that chugs you up steep Mt Washington to experience a 360° panoramic view.

It didn't look safe to me, and I refused to ride up in it, even for such a, supposedly, fantastic experience.

There were souvenir shops I couldn't resist, where I purchased magnets and a desk set for Sandy.

The Basin was an interesting twist of nature, a huge granite stone residing within the Pemigewasset River. It is like a cylinder and as the water rushes through, it creates a whirlpool. I honestly don't remember seeing it but, that is what the sign said.

We were still on the scenic Kancamongua Highway. To our right we could see valleys with mountains towering behind them. To our left was Clark's Trading Post  with a sign reading Trained Bears. We stopped, I guess, to stretch and walk a bit. We weren't interested in the poor bears.

Heading back to camp, I figured we had traveled 102 miles on that scenic highway.

It was still raining, so we pulled stakes and drove to a Tourist Cabin for the night.

It was clean, dry, and had a shower with hot and cold running water. I was enjoying such luxury. We decided not to go out again, so had dinner in the camper. Miriam, being a miracle worker with leftover food, served up a very delicious dinner. We were heading home tomorrow! I was ready.

In the morning we had a better look at our cozy cabin. It was clean, one room and bath. There were two beds, but no chairs. There was a deck and an open fireplace and picnic table. We could hear the babbling brook nearby.

It had rained hard during the night and the wind as strong. We were glad we could sleep inside.

When I went out with my gear, I discovered I had a very low tire. Fortunately, I had a tire pump in the trunk. I hooked it up to the cigarette lighter and soon had the tire ready to go. After a pancake breakfast at Mc Donald's, we were on Rt 9 heading for Brattleboro, VT. We stopped there for lunch. Maurice bit his tongue, while eating his salad and had trouble stopping the bleeding.

Miriam took the wheel, when we got back on the road; interstate 91 to Hartford, CT.

It was easy traveling until we came to the outskirts of Hartford. From Springfield to Waterbury the traffic was unbelievable. Miriam was easy to follow and we made good time getting through the congestion. We arrived at Kettletown State Park around 4:00.

It was a pretty park and our campsite was near the beach along Southbury River. Supper was leftover BBQ chicken, carrots, rice and applesauce.

It was a lovely warm evening. It was our last campfire, out last night together. In the morning we would be separating, taking different routes on our final lap home.

Maurice built a fire and we toasted marshmallows, making smore's with graham crackers and Hershey bars. He brought out his harmonica and played while Miriam and I sang. We had had a grand time together. Can one be sad and happy at the same time?

I was sad that it was ending. but happy to be going home. I was sure we would be camping again!

I was warm and comfortable sleeping on the ground again. I slept well. Aside from the rattling of a racoon trying to get into Maurice's cooler, nothing disturbed me.

We were up earlier, wanting to get an earlier start. We were on our way home, and had a distance to go. We were still in Connecticut.

I followed the camper to Brewster. There we stopped and said our final goodbye. M & M were going south, stopping in Philadelphia to visit Miriam's family. I continued west through New York, into Pennsylvania to York and Rt 83 south.

When I reached PA, I began hearing a thump, thump, thump, that sounded like a flat tire. Oh no, was the tire low again? I pulled over and got out. The tires all looked good.

Then, I realized it was the Pennsylvania roads. They were concrete squares with tar between them, to allow for expansion. I was so relieved. I had never changed a tire.

Once on Rt 83 I made good time and was home by 4 o'clock. Tired but happy. It had been a wonderful trip!

Chapter 21 • 1993—Family

In February, Laurie had a hysterectomy. I flew out to make sure she didn't overdo. That was easy and fun. We didn't do any traveling, just sat around and enjoyed being together. They had added a large new room, a family room, off the front room to the back. It had windows across the back, and a double sliding glass door on the side, leading out to a patio and backyard. The builders were still there working, so there was a lot of activity going on.

Laurie had set up a card table in the front room. She had gotten a new kind of jigsaw puzzle and wanted us to put it together. It was certainly a challenge for it was made of styrofoam and when finished, would be 3 dimensional. We had no idea what to expect, but when finished it was a lovely castle.

As I said, we mostly just sat around. But I did like to be busy. Early on, I had decided each trip, I would clean out their refrigerator. So, I did just that. I know they appreciated it and it was something I could do without disrupting anybody.

I did the same for Rick & Eileen when I visited them.

Dick & Vi Sopko made their spring visit in May. They were now arriving by plane, which meant I was now doing all the driving. That was more than fine with me and Dick said he enjoyed being chauffeured.

Also, they were happy to leave the travel plans up to me. I planned the trips and was their tour guide.

Now, I can't remember the sequence of each place we visited. We didn't go to Ocean City this time, but headed north, to Aberdeen and the Aberdeen Proving Ground and on to Havre de Grace. I have a photo of Dick & Vi standing in the doorway of a Bread & Breakfast near Longwood Gardens. It is dated May 1993. I don't know if it was at the beginning of the trip or at the ending. I do remember staying there. I remember, Vi was not a bit enthused about that. She was used to hotels & motels. I thought it would be fun, something different. It was fun! The couple that ran it also had a Flower Farm. I enjoyed the breakfast.

Men are usually interested in army stuff, and since Dick had served in the army in WWII, I thought we should visit the US Army Ordnance

Museum at the Aberdeen Proving Ground. It was interesting and when we walked around admiring the heavy army equipment Dick remembered driving one of these. Of course, we had to do a photo shoot. We proceeded north to Havre de Grace, where the mighty Susquehanna River empties into the upper Chesapeake Bay. We had lunch at a small restaurant where we could see the bridge that carried both the Amtrak and Rt 40 traffic across the river.

We explored the city, stopping to see the lighthouse, admiring the architecture, buying postcards. Wherever I traveled I bought postcards to send to my children & grandchildren.

Mother is 95.

We had celebrated Mother's 95th birthday in March. She was feeling her age. She was getting old and her body was wearing out. She was no longer able to use the walker and was pretty much bed bound. She wasn't speaking either, just nodding yes or no. It was sad to see her like that. She was always in good spirits, though. She still had her sense of humor. She was wearing Depends which were no problem during the day, but at night she would tear them up and Charlotte would find the bed wet in the morning. We tried to think of ways to keep her fingers from ripping up the Depends. We tied the openings of her night gown sleeves shut; we stuffed a garden glove so there were no fingers and had her wear them to bed. We tried everything we could think of. Still, each morning, Charlotte would find the bed wet and full of cotton stuff and Mother with a glint in her eyes as if to say, "Fooled you, I did it again!"

Chapter 22 • Trip to Adirondack Mountains

"Keep your face always toward the sunshine, and shadows will fall behind you." — Unknown

Camping with M & M, August 21, to 28, 1993

When I think about our trip to the Adirondack Mountain, it is the stressful snafu we encountered at the George Washington Bridge that immediately comes to mind. It was very stressful and left me under the weather the next day.

But first, let me tell you about getting there. I was up early that Saturday morning. I had packed my camping gear the day before. That included my CB for communicating while driving (no cell phones), my small tent, folding camp cot, folding camp stool, lamp, folding chair and of course sleeping bag and extra pad and blanket. There was just my suitcase and cooler to put in the car. A quick bite to eat and I was on my way. I was to rendezvous with Maurice and Miriam, who were driving north from Salisbury, at a rest stop on Rt295 just off the Delaware Memorial Bridge.

It was an easy drive, stopping to pay a $2 toll at Key Bridge, and $1 toll at the Delaware Memorial Bridge, where Maurice and Miriam were waiting for me. After checking out the CB, to make sure we were connecting, we were on the road, heading north to the Palisades, on the Hudson River. We must see the Palisades! Maurice insisted it would be well worth seeing. That meant taking a route near and around New York City.

Well, this is where the trouble began. Traffic was slow so Maurice was able to ask directions. We were in the wrong lane. We were in the express lane, taking us across the George Washington Bridge into New York City. We needed to get into the third lane over. I put my right signal light and began, aggressively, inching my way into the next lane and then the next lane and finally the third lane. All the while keeping the camper in view. I was worried I would lose it and would end up in the city. What would I do? We would lose contact and I would just have to find my way back home. Oh my!

The camper, being high, I was able to follow it. Inch by inch, we cut into traffic and finally reached the exit to the Palisade Parkway. I was a nervous wreck. I hoped the Palisades were worth it.

There were 3 lookout points along the Parkway and Maurice wanted to stop at them all. At the first, we turned off and drove down a snakelike, steep road to a public beach and marina. From there we had a good view of the New York City skyline and the George Washington bridge. We took pictures.

At Point lookout, we could see the rock formations that gave it the name of Palisades. The sun wasn't right for a good picture, but I snapped one anyway. Palisades are high on the hill, in the distance.

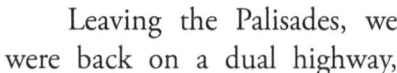

Leaving the Palisades, we were back on a dual highway, heading for our next campground. I don't remember what dual highway, but suddenly Maurice realized we were driving west, and should have been going east. I figured we would drive to the next exit and get back on the east bound road. He stopped and pulled over to the side of the road. He didn't call me on the CB, so I figured he was checking maps and would drive to the next exit, cross over and head back on the east lanes.

OH NO! In amazement, I watched him turn left, cross the highway, the median strip and down the highway going east. What could I do but follow? Fortunately, there were no other cars and.... no cops. That big brother of mine was always full of surprises!!

Harriman State Park was a welcome site. At the entrance, a sign read "no vacancy," but on inquiring, we were able to get the last campsite, #220, near Stony Point Beaver Pond. You can imagine the people and the noise of a full campground. The bathrooms showed heavy use.

After a good supper of stirfried veggies, and delicious black grapes, we walked down to the Lake, where it was quiet and peaceful. The lake, shimmering in the setting sun, was pretty. Tomorrow we would go to West Point.

Sunday, August 22.

I awoke to a lovely, sunny, hot day, but my stomach wasn't feeling so hot. The stress of the day before was taking its toll. I was having off and on stabbing pain, that eased when

I was sitting. I did ask Maurice to do the driving that morning.

After a leisurely breakfast, we drove to West Point Military Academy. It dates back to the Revolutionary War, and sits high on the banks of the Hudson River. We stood on those banks and were awed by the view of the River.

We stood, where, during the Revolutionary War, the army stretched a heavy chain across the river, preventing the English from sailing down to New York Harbor. Huge iron links of the chain and an anchor were on display there.

We walked around the campus, enjoying its beauty and history. Did you know this was where George Washington established the badge of the Purple Heart for the wounded? Did you know Mc Arthur was a superintendent there, at one time?

We toured the chapel. It was another dark chapel, like Princeton. I wasn't impressed.

The Golden Arches are always visible when looking for a lunch stop. M & M had worked up an appetite but I only wanted a muffin. Thus satisfied, we filled up with gas and headed back to camp. It was time to move on.

We followed the Hudson River, north, winding up the mountains. There was one lookout area that gave a spectacular panoramic view of the Hudson River Valley. I took several pictures on my panoramic camera, but somehow the true beauty of the valley is lost in the camera.

We arrived at the Coast to Coast Camp around 7:00. It is an organization with camps located all over the U.S. M & M are members. These camps are usually nicer and have more amenities than many camps. There is often a Lodge with rooms to rent and a dining room. At each campsite there is an electric hook up.

This camp was the Rondout Valley Resort. We quickly hooked up and set up my tent.

I had soup and crackers for supper and was in bed by 8:00. All I needed was a good night's rest and I would be fine in the morning.

Monday, August 23

Oh what a beautiful morning! I slept wonderfully and awoke to warm sunshine. I felt well and was all set for the next adventures. M & M were not up so I wandered around thinking about our plans for tomorrow. We would probably use this campsite as our focal point and take trips from here.

The bath house was nice and clean with hot showers available. There was noone else up and moving, so I took my time, luxuriating in a long hot shower. In peace and quiet.

Just as I predicted, after breakfast we headed out, in my car, for Ice Cave Mt.

We thought we would never get there. The road was rocky, steep, and very narrow in places. At the entrance was a tool gate where we paid $6 to drive to the caves. We bought the audio tour guide and continued on our way. There were pullover places to stop and enjoy the scenery. We found some huckleberries and picked some to eat. *(Memories of summers at Lake Shore40)*

  At the top of the mountain was a lake. Unusual for a lake to be on the top of a mountain. On the way down we stopped to walk the Ice Cave Trail. We hadn't gone very far when Miriam stumbled and hurt her knee. She needed to go back, but Maurice and I continued on. It was an interesting half mile trail.

The rock formations were carved by glaciers 30 million years ago. There were shallow crevasses and some that were deep like caves. One was like a tunnel. As we walked a catwalk we could see snow at the bottom of the crevasse. We were warned that it was a rough trail, and it was. We did have to go slow and watch our step.

On the way back to our campsite we stopped at the Walker Valley Vineyards. It was really a pretty place. It was located on a hill, and the hillside was covered with rows and rows of grape vines. The scene was enhanced by a pond at the base of the hill. I bought a bottle of wine for my friends Jackie and Scott.

We stopped in Ellenville when we spied a Burger King. There we indulged in a butter pecan milkshake. It was really good!

Our curiosity was piqued when we saw a strange castlelike building with turrets and all. We detoured to investigate and discovered it was the House of Correction. We didn't linger.

It was when we walked around the camp that I realized this Coast to Coast camp had all the amenities of a resort. A stream ran through it with several ponds. There was a swimming pool, a recreation center where breakfast and lunch are served from 9am to 9pm, and a playground for children. There was a special room where adults could read, play cards, or just sit and get away from the turmoil.

I was really enjoying this! I had never been to any kind of resort and found it pleasant, exciting and fun.

Oh yes, there was a telephone available, so that evening we gave Charlotte a call. Mother was not doing well and we needed to keep in touch.

Sitting around an open fire, roasting hot dogs and getting all sticky from eating smores. That's the joy of camping! Then reading from the Upper Room and bed!

Tuesday August 24

I didn't sleep well, probably the raw onion on the hot dog. The morning proved to be nice, tho humid and overcast. It was 7:30 by the time I put my eyes in, had a nice shower, and dressed.

Last night, I had written postcards, so this morning I decided to walk to the office and mail them. It was not open. I seemed to be the only one stirring.

It was so quiet and peaceful. I strolled down to the bridge to watch the water gurgle under it. I meander along the stream, listening to the music of a Fairy Waterfall, as it spilled over the rocks, singing on its way. How does one describe the pleasure one feels on a morning like this? As Pooh Bear would say, "you don't describe it, you feel it". You feel close to God! One feels sorry for those living in a busy city. How do they get close to God, in all that noise and hustle and bustle?

The sleepheads finally got up. We walked up to the Coffee Shop at the Recreation Center and had breakfast. It was a nice change and the pancakes were good.

It was almost noon when we drove to High Falls. I'm confused about the history of the area. The Delaware and Hudson Canal was involved somehow. During its journey connecting the Hudson to the Delaware the water passed through 4 locks, some raising or lowering the water 12'. There was mention of hydroelectric power and an aqueduct, to carry the water across the Rondout River. We hiked the trail along the Upper Falls and the Lower Falls. We were hoping to find some ruins of the foundation of the aqueduct, but found nothing. It was a pleasant hike; cool and very scenic. We took some pictures.

Lunch, at a Burger King in Kingston, then on to the Catskill Mountains.

We were really looking forward to seeing the Catskills. As we drove up and around the mountain, there was nothing to see but forest on both sides. There were no overlook areas to stop and enjoy the scenic views. We saw no campsite or signs of camping or trails. Nothing but dense forest. We were disappointed.

Back down the mountain to Hunter, we stopped for refreshment of blueberry and apple pie alamode. It was delicious!

241

When we saw a sign indicating a road to another waterfalls, we took it. Maurice has a thing about waterfalls. The road was very steep with only one pullover to view the scenery. Sadly, there was mist over the mountain and the tree growth was high. There wasn't much to see.

After stopping at Kingston again, for ice and groceries we were back at camp ready for supper. Each campsite had an open pit for a fire. Maurice built a fire again, and we cooked turkey burgers and stewed tomatoes. Those evenings around the campfire were wonderful and special.

Maurice might pull out his harmonica and we would sing, or we would just watch the fire and recall the things we had done that day.

We ended the evening by walking to the Recreation Center and watching other campers line dancing. We were too tired to join them. It was time for a shower and bed!

Wednesday, August 25

It had rained last night and the tent floor was wet. The floor had protruded out the front and water had come in. Isn't it just such mishaps that make camping fun!!??

I packed up everything and stowed it in the car, then spread the tent out to dry,

As we were eating breakfast Maurice thought to check the CBs and discovered his was not working. That was bad! We really needed the CBs. We might lose each other without them.

We were four hours in Kingston searching for a new CB. We were really fortunate, for when we finally found one, the salesman was so helpful. He helped Maurice connect it to his cigarette lighter and outside antenna. It was a nicer CB than the old one and thinking mine might go bad too, I bought one.

We bypassed Albany and arrived at the American Camp Ground, another Coast to Coast, near Sarasota Springs. It was hilly and Maurice had a time finding a site that would have the camper sitting at a proper angle. They didn't want to keep rolling out of bed, all night.

There had to be a flat spot too, for my tent and it needed to be near the facilities. That wasn't too much to want, was it?

Finally, satisfied with the location, we set up camp. Supper, again, was one of Miriam's delicious concoctions. Then we walked up to the store and Recreation area to buy postcards, milk and ice.

It had been a long day. We settled on plans for tomorrow and hit the sack.

Thursday, August 26

I must have been really tired, for when my head hit the pillow, I zonked out and didn't get up until 8.

Miriam was having pain in her back and legs and I was working with her, using my special techniques and stretching. She said she slept better and felt better this morning. I was glad.

Maurice was cooking breakfast as we were doing our thing and it was delicious.

Scrambled eggs with leftover ground turkey, bread and jelly and a cranberrygrape drink. He was almost as good a cook as Miriam.

It was a nice day as we headed out again. It was a back road through Gansevoort, where we stopped at a post office so I could mail my cards. I couldn't resist taking a picture of a pretty little Methodist Church. It was painted green with a lovely garden in front. All morning, as we were driving along, I noticed the steeples on small churches. They were very sharp and painted different colors. I was fascinated.

Each night we discussed our route for the next day. We had read about the Champlain Canal and its working lock, and decided it would be worth seeing. On arriving there we found an old man who was the caretaker. He was eager to talk about the lock, pointing out

the lovely landscaping on both sides of the canal. He was very proud of the well kept lawn, flowers and a picnic table that he maintained. He explained that we were looking at the new lock, built in 1950, and then showed us the wooden remains of the old lock.

As we were standing there, we watched a work boat enter the lock. It apparently had found a drifting tree and was towing it out of harm's way. The lock closed, the water was raised to the higher level, the upper gate opened and the boat went on its way. The water might raise 102' and lower 85'. Fascinating!!

Have you been to Gettysburg National Military Park? It was a Civil War battle ground. Sarasota State Historical Park was much the same. but that battle was fought in 1776, during the Revolutionary War.

Upon entering the Park, we picked up an audio tour guide, then stopped at each station to read the history. The British General, Burgoyne, was attempting to get to the Hudson River and cut off the northern states

from the New England states. The American General, Gates, was holding him back. Burgoyne finally surrendered. This was the turning point in the war, Burgoyne had failed. He could not, now, sail down the Hudson and cut off the New England States.

Did you know, in this battle, Benedict Arnold had created a distraction and became a hero?

Maurice was into all that history and wanted to read every display sign. It was hot, in the 90s, and Miriam and I had sore feet, so we found a shady tree, munched on a juicy peach and waited for him. Missing lunch. Oh well!

Supper was at a Pizza Hut before locating Sarasota Springs Spa State Park. The Visitors Center was interesting and gave us a good picture of the Spa.

It boasts of having a special spring water, found in no other place. It is a mineral water that is naturally fizzy, and bubbly. People come for the mineral baths, the bottled water, and the luxury of all a spa has to offer. Here, they offered music, dancing, art and a golf course. Not my idea of a vacation.

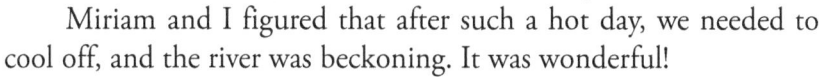

A quick drive into the city with its interesting architecture and lovely flowers everywhere, then back to camp.

Miriam and I figured that after such a hot day, we needed to cool off, and the river was beckoning. It was wonderful!

I showered and washed my hair, then walked with Miriam to the store for a Klondike bar. I bought a little battery lamp for my tent.

As was our routine we sat in the camper and planned for the next day. We would find a new C to C Camp and hunker down for a relaxing weekend.

Friday, August 27

It was 7:30 and hot and humid as we began the day. Miriam had had a bad night. Maybe the pizza? We ate breakfast, pulled stakes and were on our way, stopping at the little town of Warrensburg for groceries. As we traveled up Rt 87, we spied a rest area with a picnic table. How lucky was that? It just happened to be lunch time, so, we pulled in, used the facilities and ate lunch.

Maurice had a list of Coast to Coast camps along our route and we were searching for one. The first on his list was no longer a Coast to Coast. The second one was full. We finally found a vacancy in an American Campground, on the Schooner River. We found a campsite right next to the river. We were all ecstatic, for we could go swimming and we could sit around the campfire and listen to the sounds of the river. It was a pretty river, too.

As soon as our camp was set up, we donned swimsuits and jumped into the river. Oooh! It felt so good! Especially after such a hot day! The river bottom was sandy covered with small pebbles, easy on the feet. It was over my head out in the middle, and as I began to swam, I became conscious of the current, carrying me down river. I had no trouble swimming back to where M & M were. We frolicked and really enjoyed ourselves.

Our lovely swimming spot was also occupied by a lady sitting in an innertube tied to a submerged log. She was rocking with the current, reading a book, while watching her children play near the shore. What an ingenious idea!

Fully refreshed, and leaving the camper, we drove into the town of Lake George. It is situated at the southern end of Lake George and is quite the tourist town. Lots of boating, parasailing and a grand amusement park.

We parked and walked around a bit. I found a souvenir store and bought a sweat shirt for me and Tshirts for Rick's family.

We saw a side road that led up into the mountains and decided to explore a bit more. I mention this trip for we passed something very funny and interesting. There was a large field with lifelike figures set up in comical scenes. One by silly looking horse. Some cows and comical figures behind him.

The other was a billygoat chasing a boy and an old woman with a broom after a cow. They were all dressed in Tyrolean costumes.

After a leisurely supper we walked up to the Lodge to call Charlotte. Craig answered the phone. Mother had just died. The Mothersitter had been with her and she had called Craig. He called the police and everyone was waiting for C & C to get home. We would call back in the morning.

We called Norman & Bev in New Jersey. Tomorrow morning, we would drive to their home and spend the night. Maurice wanted to talk to Norman about asking Wheat, a lawyer, to be the attorney to settle Mother's estate. Lots to think about!

We didn't cry. We were happy for Mother. She was no longer shriveled up, skin and bones. Thank You Lord!!

Saturday, August 28

Another hot humid day. After breakfast of cereal and peaches we were on the road again. We drove into Sarasota looking for the cheap gas station we had seen before but didn't remember where, so stopped at McDonald's for lunch. I had a salad and they had fish sandwiches; we shared a Danish, then called Norman for directions to their home.

We were soon on NY 87, heading south. We somehow took a wrong exit as we were getting onto the bypass around Albany and were headed north again. These dual highways, with all the exits, and signs pointing in all directions, can be so confusing. We turned around and headed south again. We stopped for gas and discussed which route to take into New Jersey.

Norman had given us direction, Maurice wanted to take the interstate around some city east. But I figured I'd had enough of not knowing ahead of time which lane they would be in, and which exit they would take. It wasn't easy following them, especially at intersections when traffic was heavy. So, I insisted we drive the scenic route.

We arrived at Norman's in time for dinner and found Beverly had a delicious dinner waiting for us. Beverly is a wonderful cook and does things up properlike. The grilled pork tenderloin was tender and tasty, along with corn on the cob, little red parsley potatoes, and soup. I'm afraid we couldn't fully appreciate it,for we had other things on our minds.

Maurice, Norman and I discussed the plans for the funeral, and for our trip home the next day. Norman and Bev would be traveling too.

We had called Charlotte earlier this morning and again after supper. She was terribly upset. We talked a long time.

I called Laurie too. She was so very sorry she couldn't fly home. Greg was with his Dad in Colorado and the children were in school. They are, after all, her priority.

When I went to bed around 11:30 I thought, how nice it was not to have to put toilet paper on the toilet seat before sitting on it. Funny how the mind works.

I enjoyed a nice hot shower and the large bed where I could spread out. Sheer luxury! The next morning, we drove home. It had been a fun camping trip, just cut short.

Chapter 23 • Retirement

I was 69, hadn't reached 70 yet, but I had had enough. I was ready to quit. The year before, BR&L sold out to a large consortium, Physiotherapy Associates. Working was no longer fun. I could no longer spend the time I needed with each patient.

It was BR&L, not Physiotherapist Associates, that hosted my farewell dinner, on September 16, 1993. I don't remember at which restaurant in Annapolis, but the big men Wil, Bill & Ernie were there, my co workers, one patient, can't remember her name but I remember her, and, showing up as a surprise, my son, Rick. I can't remember if there was a gift or, if so, what it was. The patient gave me 2 tickets to the Burn Bre Dinner Theater.

I do remember that. Charlotte and Wheat treated me to a dinner at Black Eyed Pea and gave me an Orchid.

I had accumulated quite a bit of money in my retirement fund (I had worked 32 years).

As I remember it was about $40,000. I could take it monthly or in a lump sum, I chose to take the lump sum and invest it. That proved to be a wise decision. I invested part of it with Alex Brown, the finance company Erv had dealt with. The other went into Mutual Funds with my nephew

Glenn Davis through Prime America. There have been a lot of changes within these companies but they are basically the same and have continued to work well with me.

That September was a busy month. A weekend was spent on Skyline Drive with Charlotte and Wheat at Big Meadow Lodge. It was a favorite retreat for them and they had booked rooms for us and their friends Hazel & Charlie Avera and Lee  Harwitz. I don't remember doing anything special. The scenery was lovely. The trees were turning to golds, reds and browns. The deer were in our front yard. Were they hoping for a handout? We did stop at several overlooks to enjoy fabulous scenery.

It was October and time for Dick and Vi to come for their annual fall visit. I was looking for-   ward to their com- ing. We always did fun things and laughed a lot. Ocean City was our destination. We checked in at our favorite place, the Dunes, where we had reserved Ocean Front rooms. What was the point of going to the ocean if you couldn't see the ocean?

There was always a balcony where we would sit and watch and listen to the crashing waves. There was a porch with rocking chairs too. It was at the end of the Boardwalk and we would often walk to the stores and restaurants.

We drove up to Lewis Delaware, took the Cape May Ferry and crossed over to Cape May. I was worried for a bit, for I get seasick. I soon discovered if I stand outside by the railing and look off into the distance, I was ok. I didn't dare look down at the water going by.

We walked around the city a bit, then drove to a beach where we found old WWII bunkers. They were of concrete, built to defend our shores during WWII. I found it very interesting that they were out in the water.

They had been built on shore but the storms and tides had washed away the beach and they were now off shore.

1993 ended with a fine Christmas celebration! First, Marge & Sandy came for our annual Christmas get together. We exchanged gifts, drank hot chocolate, ate cookies and laughed a lot.

A few days later, Maurice and Miriam came up from Salisbury to spend a few days with me. It was truly a joyous time, having them here. Why is it so special and joyous to spend time with loved ones? We didn't do anything special. Just being with them, made me feel warm and happy.

Glenn & Gail hosted the New Years Eve Celebration. It was a real treat to go to their home. Glenn had games planned as entertainment for the night, and Gail served up a delicious repast. With Champagne we toasted in the New Year.

www.ingramcontent.com/pod-product-compliance
Lightning Source LLC
Chambersburg PA
CBHW051138120626
46547CB00012B/861